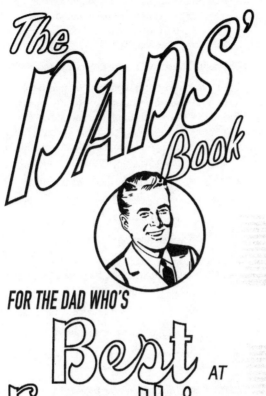

The DADS' Book

FOR THE DAD WHO'S Best AT Everything

MICHAEL HEATLEY

Michael O'Mara Books Limited

First published in Great Britain in 2007 by
Michael O'Mara Books Limited
9 Lion Yard, Tremadoc Road
London SW4 7NQ

A CIP catalogue record for this book is available
from the British Library

ISBN 978-1-84317-250-5

www.mombooks.com

Illustrations on pages 10, 15, 19, 32, 33, 34, 40, 43, 44, 45, 51, 56, 59, 66, 73,
79, 85, 86, 87, 92, 94, 98, 100, 102, 103, 106, 109, 118, 141, 151, 154
© David Woodroffe 2007

Illustration on page 89 from IMSI's MasterClips Collection

Illustrations on pages 99, 129, 146, 149 © Jupiter Images Corporation

Cover design by Angie Allison from an original design
by www.blacksheep-uk.com

Interior design and typesetting by Martin Bristow

Printed and bound in England by Clays Ltd, St Ives plc

3   5   7   9   10   8   6   4

Disclaimer: Even the best dads need to make sure that their children
are always closely supervised when engaged in any of the practical
activities mentioned in this book.

The author would like to thank Nephele Headleand, Nigel Cross
and Ian and Claire Welch for their invaluable assistance, as well as
Rod Green and everyone at Michael O'Mara Books.

Contents

CONTENTS

Introduction

Whoever said that you have to be half mad to become a Dad was only half right. You have to be completely mad. When you are a young man, you spend your time with your friends, partying in your favourite clubs or bars, watching or playing sport, unwinding at the weekends however you choose. After a hectic Saturday night out, you can roll out of bed at the crack of noon. You can read the Sunday papers starting at the sports section and use the fashion pages to catch the ketchup dripping out of your bacon sandwich. You don't want to have to wash that t-shirt, after all – you've only worn it eight or nine times.

During the week you can get out of bed and run around in a panic shaving, and eating toast in your pants, before you rush off to work. You can come home from work any time you like, having stopped off for a few beers and picked up a takeaway meal on the way. You can leave washing the dishes until later – later in the week, probably. Of course, some of this is going to change when you get married or set up home with your partner. The rest will change when the kids come along.

There will be no more long lay-ins at the weekend. Babies have to be fed and looked after and older children need to be taken to endless rounds of birthday parties or shared family outings with friends. Reading the Sunday papers is something you might get round to on Wednesday.

The morning routine needs to run like clockwork if the whole family is to get out of the house on time, so you can't be the one holding everyone else up by leaving everything to the last second. And at the end of the day, you need to be home promptly (and sober!) otherwise you won't be able to . . . join in all the fun. Having a small child fling his or her arms around your neck when you step through the front door makes you feel like the most important and special person in the whole world. And to your child, that's exactly what you are.

You won't want to miss out on the water fights or playing with floating toys at bath time. You won't want to miss out on taking your turn to read the bedtime story or that last little chat before lights out. You won't want to miss out on a single second of seeing your kids growing up, because once each precious moment you can spend together is gone, you can never get it back again.

Slushy nonsense? Not a bit of it! Having a child changes your whole life, but you must somehow find the time still to do some of the things that you have always most enjoyed. Taking a bit of time out for yourself, spending time with your old pals, will help you to be a better Dad.

If you're struggling for ideas on how to keep kids entertained, though, there are plenty of hints and tips in the pages of this book, as well as advice on how to survive the most difficult trials a Dad has to face – from the birth and the first day at school to the family holidays and teaching your youngster to drive. As practical as it is entertaining, *The Dads' Book* is essential reading for Dads everywhere, but keep it to yourself. Don't let the kids get their hands on it. You don't want them to be forewarned of the bribes and threats you might try to use on them, and you certainly don't want them to find out that the fatherly skills with which you amaze them were learned from a book. Maintain your air of manly mystery and keep this book top secret!

Most of all, though, you should use this book to give you lots of ideas about things to do to make the very most of every moment you spend with your kids. Being a Dad isn't always easy, but it can be immensely rewarding. You may have to be barking mad to become a Dad but, hey, who wants to stay sane forever?

So You're Going to Be a Dad . . .

The waiting's the hardest part for you – it's your partner who has all the really hard work to do – but waiting for the new arrival, waiting for the moment that changes your whole life, can be a real strain . . . especially if you are hanging around in a hospital maternity suite where they are all watching some crummy TV soap instead of the football.

First and foremost, don't panic. It's a frightening thought that two will soon become three, but this is the time to become a rock for your partner – not the time to disappear every night to a pub to drown your sorrows and fret over nappies.

Take an interest

Show that you are excited about the arrival of a baby and that you really do want to share in the aching joints, sweats, uncomfortable nights, expanding belly and other female body parts which generally swell, hurt, droop and get strangely distorted. You may be allowed a reprieve on the morning sickness though. Start to learn what all the baby things are and what to do with them once your baby is born. Read all the information that the midwives, doctors and hospital give your partner. You need to be on the ball.

Help choose the name. If you don't want any regrets that follow you to the grave, make sure you play an active part in choosing your baby's name. If you hate the name Horace, then say so. Alternatively, be willing to listen to other suggestions and if there isn't one name that you both desperately like then you will eventually have to compromise.

Be active

Pregnant women need to do gentle exercise. Encourage this by going along too. Walking and swimming are both good for the mum-to-be and often fathers can benefit too. Maybe you could do with losing a few pounds. You don't want to turn up at the labour ward to be asked which one of you is giving birth . . .

Get practical

Go to all antenatal appointments and scans if you can. This is your baby too and hearing its heartbeat at a routine appointment can help make the experience real for you. Scans are an excellent way to show you what's about to happen and it's also exciting. Equally, antenatal classes are informative. Dilating to ten centimetres is terrifying for any woman – especially when they show her at the class what that actually looks like – so make sure you stay supportive and comforting.

Be on standby

If your baby's due date is fast approaching, your partner will have already packed her bag ready for hospital. Make sure you know where it's kept and what to put in at the last minute if necessary. Also make sure that you are available on the phone at any time, or that someone can get a message to you immediately, if you are not. Once you get the call, get home quickly and safely and do everything you can to help your partner. Once you both decide it's time to go to the hospital, put the bag in the car – and, whatever you do, don't go into a blind panic and drive off without your partner!

In labour

Do what your partner tells you. Don't talk. Listen. Be supportive. She will probably want you to rub her back. Do this until she screams that you are irritating her. Do what your partner tells you and don't be surprised if she gives you some verbal abuse in the heat of the moment. Don't be tempted to give her an earful in return.

The aftermath

Be supportive. Hold your baby for the first time. Be supportive. Phone family. Be supportive. Phone friends. Be supportive. Hold your baby some more. Be supportive. Go home and collapse.

If this doesn't help, try the following websites:

www.pregnancy.about.com
www.babycentre.co.uk
www.thinkbaby.co.uk
www.epregnancy.com

Delivery Room Tips

Dads-to-be are expected to play their part in the operating theatre these days. You don't have to get involved in any of the messy stuff and no one expects you to be running the show, but you should try to make yourself an asset, rather than a liability

It's not about you

Giving birth is not about fathers – you did your bit months ago! You don't deliver the baby; you are in a supporting role. Get used to it.

Turn off your mobile

Your attention must be focused on your partner. Turn off your phone and certainly don't while away the time playing games on it – you'll be turning it red hot later.

No eating

If you really have to feed your face, it's best to excuse yourself and eat outside. You will need your energy, so eat well beforehand, but not so much that you throw up or faint at the first sight of a little blood or gore.

Don't monopolize the TV

If the delivery room is equipped with a TV and a VCR/DVD, bring movies she will be interested in watching.

Don't yell!

It's important to encourage her to push, but don't overdo it. Birth really hurts, even with the pain medication she's taking, so don't go over the top. Remember you are at the side of a woman giving birth, not at the side of a football pitch.

Don't complain

If you're tired or fed up with standing around, keep it to yourself. Your pain doesn't measure up to hers.

Bring a camera

The mum-to-be will expect the dad-to-be to have pictures or video when the dust has settled.

Use the camera sensibly

Check with your partner beforehand to find out what she does and does not want photographed, and with the hospital to make sure they have no objections.

Be supportive

How she decides to have the child is her decision, so don't pressure her to take/not take pain medication. A father's role during the labour and delivery process is to support his partner. Make sure she's comfortable, and gets what she wants.

Check the baby's head

If you see the number 666 anywhere, it's a bad sign.

Father Says . . .
Small children disturb your sleep,
big children your life.
YIDDISH PROVERB

Bringing Baby Home

Be prepared

With nine months' notice, there is no excuse for not being prepared! Hopefully you'll have the nursery and all necessary baby equipment ready to use.

Family pets

It may be difficult for your pet to cope with a new family member. Your dog or cat is used to being the centre of attention. Your new baby will demand a lot of your time and energy, so you should gradually get your pet used to spending less time with you. If your pet is particularly attached to the mother-to-be, another family member should try to develop a closer relationship with the animal.

Shopping

Make sure you have plenty of supplies; you won't have time to keep going shopping.

Your partner will need lots of nutrients to boost her energy levels, especially if breastfeeding. Make sure you have plenty of fresh fruit and vegetables. Freezers are excellent for stocking up on pre-cooked meals. Friends or relations who ask if they can help, can cook and freeze some meals for you.

Household tasks

Ensure the house is clean and tidy and that all laundry is washed and ironed. You won't want to be running around doing the chores when you could be spending time with the new arrival.

The day before

Bring home as much as possible from hospital. Things like flowers, gifts and cards will make your home look welcoming and bringing them home early means that they don't take up space in the car when you're transporting mother and baby.

Get a good night's sleep

Save the night out with the lads to wet the baby's head until later – there'll be plenty of opportunity to celebrate the birth! Instead, enjoy the last full night's sleep you'll going to have for some time. Caring for your new addition and your partner will

Father Says . . .
I remember the time I was kidnapped
and they sent a piece of my finger to my father.
He said he wanted more proof.
RODNEY DANGERFIELD

take up every minute of your day, so ensure you have recharged your batteries.

Leaving hospital

Mums-to-be generally pack clothes for the trip home before going to hospital, unless it was an unexpected early arrival. Check with your partner if there are any items needed for the journey, such as baby hats or extra blankets. Find out where her loose-fitting clothes are kept – she won't appreciate you turning up with her tight-fitting jeans just yet!

Ask the experts

If you have any questions about caring for your baby or the aftercare of your partner, check with the nursing staff. They will have all the answers to put your mind at ease. Make sure you have all necessary emergency contact numbers should you need to call.

Car trip

The most important item for the trip home is a proper child car seat. Check the legal safety requirements and practise fitting the seat – if in doubt, have your installation checked. Even for a short trip, it's never safe for one of you to hold your baby in your arms or to put a carrycot on a back seat.

Visitors

New mums need plenty of rest, so don't hesitate to use the answering machine to screen your calls. Dads can be helpful by discouraging too many visitors in the first few days – you may not believe it now, but life will eventually become less hectic.

Choosing a Name

It's a new dad's biggest headache – what name to choose for the new arrival? Your partner will certainly have her own ideas about names, but you need to be prepared to participate in the discussion, otherwise it looks like your ducking out. But where do you start? Here's a handy guide to help end the headscratching:

Does it sound right?
Saying the name aloud is one of the best tests.

How does it sound? Melodious? Harsh?

How does it go with your surname? Longer first names work better with shorter surnames, and vice versa.

Avoid a first name ending in a vowel if your surname starts with one, as the names tend to run together.

Avoid rhyming Christian and surnames.

Avoid puns: remember your child has to live with your choice for the rest of his or her life.

Uniqueness
An unusual name will make your child stand out from the crowd, but may cause problems with pronunciation or spelling. Consider choosing a familiar first name if your surname is unusual, and vice versa.

Bear in mind that 'charming' names that suit a toddler will embarrass a teenager and no one wants to make a potential employer start sniggering at a job interview.

Relatives
Don't let relatives push you into choosing a name you don't like. You never know who you might offend by choosing one name

over another. Family disputes are well worth avoiding, while aunts and grandparents names, however well-loved, may be dated.

Ancestry and heritage

You may wish to reflect your family's heritage or religion in your choice of names. First-born sons are also often named after their fathers, or take a middle name from their mother.

Meaning

Names all have meanings and this is always worth thinking about.

Initials

Consider the initials your child will be stuck with for the rest of their lives, and make sure they don't spell out any unwanted nickname.

Oddball choices

No matter how fanatical a football supporter you are, avoid adding the names of your team to your child's – unless you want to end up in the tabloids!

Most Popular Names

What you name your baby is one of the most important decisions you make for your child. The choices of others may help you make it.

Girls

1 **Jessica** was first used by Shakespeare in his play *The Merchant of Venice* and is based on the biblical Jesca, from the Hebrew *Yiskah* ('God beholds').

2 **Emily** comes from the Roman surname *Aemilius*, which was originally from the Latin word *aemulus*, meaning 'rival'.

3 **Sophie** is a form of Sophia, from the Greek word *sophos*, meaning 'wise'.

4 **Olivia** is from the Latin word *oliva*, meaning 'olive'.

5 **Chloë** comes from the Greek *Khloe*, meaning a 'green shoot' on a plant or flower and also means 'blooming'.

6 **Ellie** is the English short form of Helen, from the Greek *Helene* ('torch' or 'light') or *selene*, meaning 'moon'.

7 **Grace** originally comes from the Latin *gratia*, meaning 'thanks'.

8 **Lucy** is the feminine form of Lucius, derived from the Latin *lux*, meaning 'light'.

9 The name **Charlotte** is the feminine form of Charles, meaning 'strong' and was made popular by Queen Charlotte in the eighteenth century.

10 **Katie** is the English short form of Katherine, from the Greek *katharos*, meaning 'pure'.

Boys

1. **Jack** developed as a pet form of John, via the nickname Jankin, but is now a name in its own right. John is originally from the Hebrew name *Yochanan* meaning 'God is gracious'.

2. **Joshua** comes from the Hebrew *Yehoshua,* via the Greek *Iesos*, meaning 'God is salvation'.

3. **Thomas** is the Greek form of the Aramaic name *Teoma*, literally meaning 'twin'.

4. **James** comes from the Latin *Iacomus*, which is from the Greek *Iacobus* and the Hebrew *Yaakov*, which could be from the Hebrew words *aqev* or *aqab*, meaning 'heel' or 'supplanter'.

5. **Oliver** comes from the Latin *olivarius* ('olive tree').

6. **Daniel** is derived from the Hebrew name *Daniyyel*, meaning 'God is my judge'.

7. **Samuel** is another Biblical name. *Shemu'el*, which means 'God has heard', comes from the Hebrew *shama*, meaning 'heard' and *el*, meaning 'God'.

8. **William** means 'resolute protector' and comes from the Old High German name *Willahelm* – *wil*, meaning 'desire' and *helm*, meaning 'helmet' or 'protector'.

9. A medieval form of Henry, **Harry** is from the Germanic *Heimerich* – *heim*, meaning 'home' and *ric*, meaning 'power' or 'ruler'.

10. **Joseph** comes from the Hebrew *Yosef*, meaning 'God will give', via the Greek *Iosephos* and the Latin *Iosephus*.

Wacky Celebrity Baby Names

Famous dads think they can get away with anything – please don't try this at home, for your kids' sake!

Daughters of Simon and Yasmin Le Bon
Amber Rose Tamara
Saffron Sahara
Tallulah Pine

Children of Coldplay's Chris Martin and actress Gwyneth Paltrow
Apple Blythe Alison
'It sounded so sweet and it conjured such a lovely picture for me, apples are so sweet and they're wholesome and it's biblical and I just thought it sounded so lovely and . . . clean!'
said Gwyneth

Moses Bruce Anthony
The first name can be explained by the song, 'Moses', that Chris Martin wrote for Gwyneth shortly before their secret wedding. It includes the words 'Like Moses has power over sea, so you've got power over me . . .'

First child of *Six Feet Under* actress Rachel Griffiths and Andrew Taylor
Banjo Patrick

Children of Woody Allen and Mia Farrow
Dylan Farrow (changed her name to Eliza
and is now known as Malone)
Moses Farrow (now known as Misha)
Satchel Farrow (now known as Ronan Seamus Farrow)

Daughters of Paula Yates and Bob Geldof
Fifi Trixibelle
Peaches Honeyblossom Michelle Charlotte Angel Vanessa
'I hate ridiculous names, my weird name has haunted me all
my life.' – Pixie Geldof

Daughter of Paula Yates
and Michael Hutchence
Heavenly Hiraani Tiger Lily

The five sons of former Boxing Champion
George Foreman
George
George
George
George
George
And don't forget his two daughters,
Freeda George and Georgetta

Daughters of TV design guru
Anna Ryder Richardson and Colin MacDougall
Ibi Belle
Dixie Dot

Son of actress Nicolas Cage
Kal-el Coppola (the supposed birth name of Superman)

Daughters of Demi Moore and Bruce Willis
Rumer Glenn
Scout LaRue
Tallulah Belle

Children of Frank Zappa
and Adelaide Gail Sloatman
Moon Unit
Dweezil
Ahmet Emuukha Rodan (named after Ahmet Ertegun,
one of two brothers who founded and headed Atlantic
Records)
Diva Thin Muffin

Daughter of former Sporty Spice Mel B
and dancer Jimmy Gulzar
Phoenix Chi

Daughters of chef Jamie and Jules (Juliette) Oliver
Poppy Honey
Daisy Boo

Daughter of Brad Pitt and Angelina Jolie
Shiloh Nouvel (means 'Messiah' or 'peaceful one')

Daughter of Tom Cruise and Katie Holmes
Suri (means 'pointy nose' in Todas but parents like the
meanings 'princess' and 'red rose' better!)

Son of Angie and David Bowie
Zowie Bowie (for a while when he was younger,
he was known as Joe or Joey. He now prefers to be known
as Duncan Jones, his father's real last name.

Double Trouble – Intriguing 'Facts' about Twins

There's only one thing as scary as the news you're expecting twins – and that's the many myths and misconceptions that circulate about twins. Let's examine the fact and fiction about multiple births

It's twice as hard to raise twins

Not necessarily. In some ways, having more than one at a time is actually easier than having several kids of different ages. Twins are natural companions for each other, serving as playmates and taking some of the burden off mum and dad.

One is good and one is evil

There are times when one twin will try to attract parental attention by being a 'little angel' when the other is playing up, but no child is all good or all bad.

They always need a caesarean birth

While there are risks associated with multiple births that can make caesarean sections a safer option, not all twins are born that way. The chance increases with the number of babies, and quadruplets or quintuplets are almost always delivered in the operating room. But some obstetricians even have a lower c-section rate with twins than with single births!

Twins should be separated in school

Although schools may say otherwise, there is no evidence that indicates that twins do better if placed in separate classrooms, or worse if kept together. Some studies have even concluded that separation can actually be detrimental to their educational experience. Several factors should be considered, including the dynamic of the children's relationship and their individual learning styles.

Families with 'multiples'
(twins and above) get a discount

Sadly, that's not always so. Occasionally, schools or activities will offer a discount – say ten or twenty per cent – for a second child. But, as multiples become more common, such breaks are the exception and not the rule.

Twins are always the best of friends

Although the bond between twins is unique and special, they enjoy friendships and relationships with other kids just like singleton siblings and aren't automatically exclusive pals.

Twins are always in competition

Sibling rivalry can kick in as with any family, but as twins develop their own individual identity they won't necessarily feel compelled to contrast themselves with their twin.

The older twin is a leader,
the younger is a follower

Nothing much happens in those few minutes, or sometimes seconds, between births that could impact personality. If a firstborn multiple exhibits leadership traits, he or she would probably have developed those inclinations in any case.

Twins have ESP

Intriguing, but false. We've all heard stories of twins finishing each other's sentences and feeling each other's pain, but it's a phenomenon scientists say any two people – husbands/wives, close siblings or good friends – can exhibit.

They look so similar no one can tell them apart

Even identical twins with similar physical attributes have differences. Parents can almost always tell their children apart, and they won't forget who is who. That's not to say they won't be fooled from time to time – especially when sleep-deprived!

Your Baby's Star Sign

Getting to know your child is a joy for any Dad. This astrological guide may help you get ahead of the game.

Capricorn (December 22–January 19)

Inside every Capricorn child is a wise old soul with a sense of responsibility. Don't let this interfere with the natural stages of childhood. Encourage balance, ease, laughter and risk-taking. Encourage realistic goal-setting, reinforcing the value of not only the result but what is learned along the way.

Aquarius (January 20–February 18)

A free spirit, the young Aquarian thrives on change and surprise, not routine. Aquarians are original thinkers, so give your child space to explore and you'll be surprised by what he or she invents. But a unique mental perspective can create feelings of isolation and loneliness, so your child will need your help to find his or her way socially.

Pisces (February 19–March 20)

Pisces are highly sensitive children who require love, care and closeness in order to feel safe in this world. Pisces children appreciate order, structure and assistance in setting goals. Gently reinforce steps toward greater independence, aware that your son or daughter may have fears that block progress, and encourage communication.

Aries (March 21–April 19)

Aries children are assertive and independent, seeking new experiences. He or she will be outgoing, competitive and excited about the world. Don't be surprised if your youngster is in a hurry to walk, so provide a safe environment where energy can be focused and potential realized. Teach the value of completing tasks and encourage sensitivity to others.

Taurus (April 20–May 20)

Your Taurus baby thrives on affection and creature comforts. Food and a loving touch play important roles in meeting this sign's primary need: to feel a consistent sense of security in the world. A serene environment with dependable routines helps your child enjoy each day. To help develop positive personality traits and fulfil innate potential, let your Taurus child explore at his or her own pace.

Gemini (May 21–June 20)

Mentally alert, responsive, and incredibly entertaining, Gemini children have a capacity for early mental and social development. Avoid overstimulating this active mind; storytelling can help your Gemini child to relax. It is typical for a Gemini child to have too many interests going on at the same time, sometimes leading to a sense of distraction that can be a handicap in school. Create an atmosphere that supports concentration and inquisitiveness, and if he or she asks endless questions show them how to find the answers.

Cancer (June 21–July 22)

The young Cancerian is sensitive, imaginative, and aware of others' feelings. Hold your child as much as possible, letting them know that you intend to create a safe place as long as need be; it'll be clear when the time comes to help your child build a separate identity and greater self-confidence. Encourage your child to take creative risks. Although he or she relies mostly on intuition, memory will play an important part in success at school. Your child appreciates structure and guidelines from positive authority figures.

Leo (July 23–August 22)

Confidence and self-respect are Leo traits; with these, your child can see the potential for creative self-expression and leadership. You can cultivate these attributes by providing honest feedback, praise and attention. Be aware that competition for attention among family members can create complications in future relationships, so be understanding rather than indifferent lest emotions escalate until your young Leo gets your attention!

Virgo (August 23–September 22)

Virgo children are acutely observant, bright, alert to subtle patterns, and want to understand how everything works. Only the highest standard is the model to emulate. Virgo kids are sensitive to criticism and attached to the idea of being right. As a parent, you should try to show acceptance and forgiveness. Virgo children require routines to feel safe and are happy to help out Mum and Dad around the house.

Libra (September 23–October 22)

This child is eager to please and tends to follow role models. Overly sensitive to harsh atmospheres, your little Libra will appreciate beauty, balance and serenity. He or she will be loving and responsive and in many cases will assume the role of the peacemaker. Librans have a natural inclination toward theatre, music, art, romance and happily-ever-after stories. As they grow older, their need for beauty, balance and fair play becomes a motivation to enhance their lives and the lives of others.

Scorpio (October 23–November 21)

A Scorpio is inquisitive and not easily coerced into doing what others expect. You're better off winning their cooperation rather than going head-to-head with one; a predominant characteristic of this sign is a phenomenal amount of willpower. Betrayal is not quickly forgotten. The trusting child will share private feelings and will count on you to keep those secrets and respect their personal likes and dislikes. With such a deep connection, this child will enjoy a close parental relationship.

Sagittarius (November 22–December 21)

Your Sagittarius baby will be restless and inquisitive, filled with enthusiasm, and an inborn optimist. Keep him or her entertained with the wonder of new experiences. Once able to walk, your youngster will be out the door and around the block before you know it! Teach your child to deal with the negative as well as the positive, though he or she won't easily accept 'no' and 'can't'. Things usually come without much effort for the Sagittarian. A sport or other activity requiring effort and self-discipline is a good foundation for future success.

Father Says . . .

There isn't a child who hasn't gone out into the brave new world who eventually doesn't return to the old homestead carrying a bundle of dirty clothes.

ART BUCHWALD

Ten Lamest Excuses

1 'With everything else you asked me to do today, I forgot.'

2 'I only went for one beer but they wouldn't let me leave.'

3 'I thought you'd already done it.'

4 'It was the dog.'

5 'I did try, but you know I'm no good at it.'

6 'The washing machine ate my socks.'

7 'The car broke down and when I got there it was shut.'

8 'The battery on my phone must have died.'

9 'Traffic.'

10 'Your mother came round, the kids were playing up, the microwave wasn't working, I couldn't find the tin opener, the phone never stopped ringing and the dog decided to pee on the carpet, so I just didn't get round to it.

Father Says . . .
Some people have got advice (about fatherhood), some people have got horror stories. I like people that look you in the eye with a glow and say, 'It's gonna be cool.'
RUSSELL CROWE

How to Avoid Changing a Nappy

The gunk that goes into the top end of a baby is pretty disgusting, but it's got nothing on the stuff that comes out the other end. How many times have you avoided changing the nappy on someone else's child because you know it's going to be a horrible job? Let's make no bones about it, it isn't in any way pleasant, but ask anyone what changing a nappy is like and they will all tell you, 'It's different when it's your own baby . . .' They're all liars. The only difference is that when it's your own kid's poo, you have to deal with it so often that you simply get used to it.

If you really can't bear the thought of getting stuck in, you need preparation and mental agility to be able to come up with a justifiable reason why your partner should take on the task . . . a task that she's probably undertaken several times already that day. Keep an eye – or more usefully a nose – on your child and, once you know the deed has been done, put your plan into action. Here are a few suggestions to get you thinking in the right mode:

❶ Offer to ring her mother to bring her up to date with the day's events. Your partner will be too stunned to think there is an ulterior motive – just don't overuse this one!

2. If there's a job around the house that you've been getting nagged to do, start doing it. Your partner will put up with changing the nappy if it means that the spare room is redecorated or the fence is mended.

3. Make sure any other children are entertained. Either sit down with them and do their homework; play a game with them; or take them to the park.

4. Don't just volunteer to do a household chore, actually get up and start doing the washing up, the dishes or the ironing.

5. If you're really on top of your game, then you will have noticed the situation before your partner realizes what your child has done and you'll have popped out to the supermarket to do the shopping.

6. Feign serious illness.

It's all about paying attention and trying to stay one step ahead. Always carry on thinking of new excuses because you've got between two and three years of this so you need plenty of variation!

How To Change A Nappy

If all else fails, you may actually have to roll up your sleeves and change the nappy yourself. Let every whiff that scorches your nasal hair be a reminder to you to think up some more convincing excuses for next time! In the meantime, here's how it's done . . .

Firstly, ensure your baby is laid on a flat, soft surface, ideally on a waterproof changing mat. Babies should never be left unattended unless in their cot or pram, since they can roll over and fall from a high surface.

1. Wash your hands well.

2. Remove any jewellery that could scratch the baby.

3. Make sure you have everything ready to clean and change the baby.

4. Put a couple of safe toys in the baby's sight for entertainment, although this may also be an ideal time to remember those nursery rhymes.

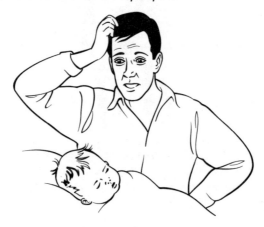

5. Remove the dirty nappy. As you take off the soiled/wet nappy, hold the baby gently by the ankles and lift the hips. Throw away the dirty nappy.

6. Wipe the baby clean and dry well.

7. Apply cream to prevent nappy rash.

8. Unfold a new nappy, lift the baby's hips again and slip it underneath.

9. Bring the front of the nappy up between the baby's legs.

10. Fasten the adhesive tapes as tightly as appear comfortable.

11. Dress baby.

12. Wash your hands again.

You may find yourself all 'fingers and thumbs' at first, but after a short while, you'll become extremely good at it. And that's just as well – after all, it'll be happening at least five times a day, not counting the night changes.

The above, of course, only applies to disposable nappies. If your partner has 'gone green' and decided to use the re-usable towelling nappies, brush up on your avoidance techniques or feign death.

Father Says . . .
A baby-sitter is a teenager who gets two dollars
an hour to eat five dollars' worth of your food.
HENNY YOUNGMAN

What to Do
While Mum's Away

If your partner has to go away for a few days (perhaps on business or maybe even to produce another new arrival) it may be time to start grovelling to your mother-in-law and taking back all those things you said when you thought she wasn't listening. Alternatively, you could be a man about it and take on the challenge of looking after your offspring with the aid of our survival guide.

Prepare yourself
Start watching what your partner does while she's still at home. Learn the ropes and if you're very clever, start joining in. You might find washing the dishes or doing the Hoovering a chore, but bath time, reading stories and pillow fights (best to leave this until mum has actually gone) are all fun.

You don't want to have the attitude that if you go to the supermarket and do it really badly (by forgetting the bread and baby's formula, etc.) that you won't have to do it again. Chances are you will be made to do it again and again until you get it right. Also, it's the little ones in your life that will suffer if you mess up while mum's away.

Learn military precision
No household can operate effectively without it. If it helps, make lists and a timetable. You need to remember that school gates normally open at 8.45 a.m. and close again at ten past three. Choir rehearsals, music lessons, ballet classes and football sessions all happen on different days. If they do, you're lucky; if they don't, make sure the car is serviced and full of petrol, the satnav is plugged in and programmed or that you

have the appropriate bus timetables. Make sure you also have directions to places you don't normally go – like the doctor and dentist. You don't want to be running around like a lunatic, carrying a child that needs medical attention, when you've got no idea where you're going.

Cooking and shopping

In the weeks prior to your partner's departure, start watching cookery programmes and note how your partner prepares a meal. Ask her to provide you with a weekly shopping list so you don't overlook any essential items. Doing the washing without any powder or liquid will be difficult and will only result in you having to make an extra journey to buy some. Plus, you'll have to do the washing all over again. Definitely seek out your local Tesco, Morrison's and Iceland. You need to feed the children a balanced diet, although there is, and should, be room for treats (but keep these to a minimum – you are not going to be a pushover).

If you don't normally feed your children certain foods, don't suddenly introduce them into their diet just because mum's away. It will add confusion – the younger the child, the more reassurance they will need while mum is not at home – plus you may get poorly tummies (spicy spare ribs are not good for toddlers) which is not nice, especially if you're a novice at dealing with sickly kids.

Father Says . . .
Being a parent is a big responsibility, one of life's greatest things . . . a pain in the arse.
NOEL GALLAGHER

Keep to the children's normal routine

Children like routines, it makes them feel safe and secure. Don't let them stay up late watching something unsuitable on TV with you. It will only lead to nightmares, tiredness, arguments and tantrums – all of which you will have to deal with. If you have older children you are lucky, as the chances are they will know exactly where to find everything, how the microwave works and where mum keeps the cleaning kit for when the cat throws up. Use this knowledge and ask for help, but don't abuse it and expect your older children to take over where mum left off.

If you do get help, always reward appropriately, perhaps by offering to let them have friends over. Make sure you will be in though and don't leave your stash of beers on show and available – otherwise what will you have to drink?

Having coped admirably with the absence of your nearest and dearest, not only will you feel elated and proud of yourself, but your partner may start to see the 'new' man in you. But be warned – this may lead to more domestic responsibilities for you in the long run and you will definitely need a holiday to get over it in the short-term.

If you are lucky, your partner (unless struck down by illness) will probably have put everything in place for you. But, be prepared for the unexpected and keep smiling . . . even if that means gritting your teeth and going to bed early.

Father Says . . .
Little children, headache; big children, heartache.
ITALIAN PROVERB

Friends and Family

How to keep your friends
and keep in with your family

As you will no doubt be aware, having a child brings about the biggest change in your life, short of being hit by a train. You will have already noticed this if you have friends who have had children. Your best mate won't be down the pub every evening getting drunk with you while watching the football, playing pool or simply hanging out. Be prepared – this *will* happen to you, too.

Staying friends

In order to deal with this change you need to cultivate relationships with your friends who already have children. Listen to the advice they can offer on how to get your toddler to sleep at night or which is the best television programme to let them watch – this will keep them entertained for a while and give you some much-needed time to do a few household chores or put your feet up and catch forty winks!

Having friends with children also means that you can arrange to do things together, allowing you to have some adult company and the kids to play together so they're not pestering you every minute. It's great fun when families get together and go out for the day, whether it's a barbecue or just a romp in the park. Your friends might also be prepared to babysit your child at their house so you can enjoy an evening out with your partner. Just remember to reciprocate or you'll find they won't offer the favour again!

While bringing up your child is a lifetime responsibility, do remember that when they have grown up and found their own independence, you will have more freedom to do things that you want to do so it's important that you have kept in touch with your friends. You won't be pulling your weight in the childcare stakes if you are out with your pals every night, but once in a while, now and again, is definitely a good idea to get some time away from the family.

Relative problems

Once you have a child, you'll find that your entire family will want to descend on you for a visit. Great-aunt Flossie will suddenly decide that, after twenty years, it's time she saw you again, time she met your partner and time she came to stay for a week or two!

While it's perfectly acceptable for the newborn's grandparents and close uncles and aunts to want to see the baby, it's only fair on your other half to be selective and limit the amount of time she has to put up with other people in the house – especially just after coming home from hospital. Of

course, she might welcome her mother visiting for a while to help once she has come home, so it's down to you to make sure that you maintain good relations with your mother-in-law . . .

Relatives will always have advice for you as a parent, whether you have asked for it or not! No matter how good a parent you are, at some point they will frown on the way you are dealing with a particular situation and come out with one of the old chestnuts like 'My mother didn't do that!' or 'It wasn't like that in my day!' Be diplomatic. Don't start arguing. Remember – the best thing about advice is that it is freely given but it doesn't *have* to be taken.

Don't forget that the fact that you now have had a child will tend to make some of your relatives feel older – especially your mum and dad. They have gone to bed one night as parents and woken up the next morning as grandparents! They probably still see you as their little boy . . .

Love thy neighbour

Whether you get on with your neighbours or not will direct how you approach your relationship with them when you have a child. If they are friendly, you are more likely to try to keep the noise down and be embarrassed if your child is having a screaming tantrum at three in the morning. If you don't get on at all, then you probably won't be too worried about disturbing their sleep!

Joking aside, whether your neighbours are your best friends or not, making a real effort to keep in with them will pay dividends in the long run. If you live in a block of flats or a terraced house where there is a degree of noise penetration, your neighbours will be far better disposed to the inevitable noise that a newborn baby can make if you have taken the trouble to butter them up a bit.

It is also far easier to ask a noisy neighbour to keep the din down when you're trying to get the baby to sleep if you have made the effort to befriend said neighbour first. Try to be a considerate, good neighbour, and you will find that your neighbour is more accepting on the odd occasion when there is a lot of noise coming from your house.

Neighbours can also become great friends to you and your children. If they have kids themselves, then your child has ready-made playmates next door and you have friends on hand with whom you can socialize.

If your neighbours are elderly, encourage your child to strike up a friendship with them. Your child will be fascinated by the stories they can recount of what life was like when they themselves were young. If they are able, they might enjoy joining you for a walk in the park or even doing a bit of babysitting now and again. If they are rather more frail, they will be comforted by the thought that someone next door cares for them and is looking out for them.

Being good to your neighbours generally means that they will be good to you, too.

Father Says . . .
Human beings are the only creatures on earth
that allow their children to come back home.
BILL COSBY

How to Make a Bow and Arrow

If you really want to be a hero to your kids and impress them with your skills as an outdoorsman, go wrestle a bear or a crocodile. Alternatively, you could show them how to make a bow and arrow. Follow these instructions and, with a bit of practice, you'll be hitting a target at twenty paces in no time. Make sure you use an old dart board or something suitable as a target though. Try this out on the cat, no matter how much you hate the thing, and you'll go from hero to zero faster than a speeding arrow. A mound of soft earth or sand in the garden will do as a target. This will also help to preserve your arrows and makes them far easier to retrieve than chasing a wounded cat.

To make your bow and arrow you will need:

◆ A wooden staff about 1.5 m long and at least as thick as your thumb. Try to find or cut a straight length with little or no knots or offshoots. Yew is the traditional bow-making wood, but you can also use oak, elm, birch or just about any other strong, healthy wood.

◆ As many straight, thin, 75 cm-lengths of wood as you would like for arrows.

◆ Some feathers (you can find them or maybe ask your local butcher) or some thin plastic card to use as flights

◆ Cord or twine

◆ Cotton thread

◆ A sharp knife

To make the bow

① To make your bow bend and spring back you need to chamfer the ends. Mark the staff 0.5 m from each end. Shave these end sections along the inside of the bow, tapering towards the tip. You don't need to shave it too thin; you should slim the bow gradually until the tips are about half as thick as the middle. Next cut a thin groove in the unchamfered outside edge of the bow. The groove needs to be about 5 cm from the end. This is where you will tie your bowstring.

② Tie the twine you are using as a bowstring to one end and bend the bow. Don't bend it too far as it will have to go further still when you are firing an arrow. Pull the bowstring taught and cut the required length.

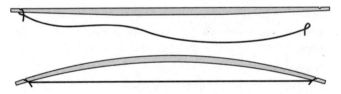

③ Make a loop in the open end of the string. Now slip this loop over the other end of the bow so that it sits in the notch. Always release the string when you are not using the bow so that the bow does not 'set' in its bent shape and lose its power.

The Arrows

① The front of an arrow needs to be heavier than the back to stop the arrow tumbling through the air. Find the mid point of the arrow by balancing it on your finger. Now you can tell which end (the shorter side) is heavier. Cut a slot in the lighter end and slide a feather in so that it sticks out on either side of the slot. This will be your flight. Wrap some cotton thread ahead of the feather and behind it to squeeze the slot and clamp the feather in place. You can use a piece of shaped plastic or card instead of a feather.

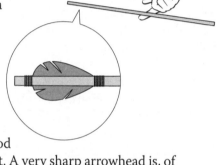

❷ If you are feeling really macho, you can make an arrowhead by pounding a piece of flint into a thin blade or carving a sliver of bone. Arrowheads can be clamped in place using the same method you used for the flight. A very sharp arrowhead is, of course, extremely dangerous. It is safer and easier just to scorch the end of the arrow over a flame to harden it and then sharpen it with a knife. It is safer still to use a piece of modelling clay on the tip.

Now you are ready for target practice. You might want to wear a glove on your bow hand to protect you from the string because it can really sting if it catches your wrist and, unless you can turn your whimpering into an effective war whoop, you're going to look pretty stupid at that point.

You can scale down the whole process to make bows for the kids. Now look up the 'Ten Best Threats' in this book to stop them from shooting you in the backside as soon as your back is turned.

You're Never Too Old . . .

Age is irrelevant when it comes to fatherhood. You might think that the older we get, the more sense we should have, but it seems that some old timers still want to be dads. Do we never learn?

The world's oldest recorded father is Australian mine worker, Les Colley, who was ninety-two years and ten months when he fathered a son, Oswald, in 1992. 'I never thought she would get pregnant so easy, but she *$@^! well did,' he told newspapers at the time, referring to his Fijian wife whom he'd met through a dating agency a year earlier. Colley died just four months short of his hundredth birthday in 1998.

In a survey by Lloyds TSB, over a third of Brits surveyed said they thought fathering a child when over the age of fifty was 'great'. Fathers Direct (the National Information Centre on Fatherhood) argues that the advantages of late fatherhood outweigh the disadvantages. 'Research shows that old fathers are three times more likely to take regular responsibility for a young child. They are more likely to be fathers by choice and this means they become more positively involved with the child. They behave more like mothers, smiling at the baby and gurgling – although young fathers are probably better at getting down on the floor for physical play.'

Dinosaur dads

Since 1980, there has been about a forty per cent increase in the number of men between thirty-five and fifty fathering children and a twenty per cent decrease in the number of fathers under thirty. Data from the UK's Office For National Statistics (ONS) reveals that in 1971 the mean age of a father at the time of his first child's birth was 27.2 years, but by 1999 this had risen to 30.1. Statistics from 1997 show that, while the majority of fathers (151,162) were in the thirty to forty age group, there were 41,459 fathers aged from forty to over sixty-five.

Des O'Connor

When he was seventy-two, singer and TV host Des O'Connor's first son, Adam Harrison Campbell (named after Des's father and partner Jodie Brooke Wilson's father's family name) was born in September 2004. This is the first child for O'Connor and singer-songwriter Jodie. For Des, however, his son's arrival makes five offspring, following his four daughters, Karen (born 1963), Tracy Jane (born 1964), Samantha (born 1968) and Kristina (born 1988) from three previous marriages.

Larry King

Aged sixty-seven, award-winning American Broadcaster Larry King became a father to his seventh child, Cannon Edward (born 2000). King married sixth wife Shawn Southwick in 1997 and adopted her son. They also have a son called Chance Armstrong (born 1999). King's other children include daughter Chaisa (born 1967) from his marriage to former *Playboy* bunny Alene Akins along with adopted son Andy (from Akin's first marriage), daughter Kelly from marriage to Mickey Sutphin and son Larry (born 1962) from an earlier relationship.

Luciano Pavarotti

Aged sixty-eight, Italian tenor Luciano Pavarotti and second wife (former assistant/secretary) Nicoletta Mantovani had twins in January 2003. Unfortunately the baby boy died following complications, with his surviving sister weighing just

3.8 lbs at birth. Alice is Pavarotti's fourth daughter following Lorenza (born 1964), Cristina (born 1964) and Giuliana (born 1976) with his first wife of thirty five years, Adua Veroni.

Hugh Hefner

Aged sixty-four, founder of *Playboy* magazine, Hugh Hefner became a father on his own birthday (9 April) to Marson Glenn in 1990 and then again on 4 September 1991 to Cooper Bradford by second wife and 1989 Playmate of the Year Kimberley Conrad. Hefner fathered two children when married to first wife Mildred 'Millie' Williams. Daughter Christie Ann (now Chairperson of Playboy Enterprises Inc.) was born 8 November 1952 and brother David Paul born 30 August 1955.

Warren Beatty

Aged sixty-three, American actor, producer and screenwriter, Warren Beatty and wife Annette Bening (his co-star in 1991 gangster film *Bugsy)* had their fourth child Ella Corrine (born 2000). Their three other children are daughters Kathlyn Elizabeth (born 1992), Isabel Ira Ashley (born 1997) and son Benjamin McLaine (born 1994).

Julio Iglesias

Aged sixty-three, Spanish singer Julio Iglesias had baby number eight on the way in 2006 with partner Miranda Rijnsburger. They already have two boys – Miguel (born 1997) and Rodrigo (born 1999) and twin girls Victoria and Cristina (born 2001). His other children include Chabeli María Isabel (born 1971) Julio José (born 1973) and famous singer Enrique Miguel (born 1975). Julio is following in his own father's footsteps. Dr Iglesias Puga became a father again at the age of eighty-nine years to Julio's half-brother Jaime. Dr Iglesias' partner Ronna Keitt was expecting their second child when he died suddenly at the age of ninety. Daughter Ruth was born on what would have been his ninety-first birthday.

Sir Paul McCartney

Aged sixty-one, former Beatle Sir Paul McCartney's fourth child, a daughter named Beatrice Milly McCartney, was born on 28 October 2003 to second wife Heather Mills. She was named after Heather's late mother Beatrice and Sir Paul's Aunt Milly.

Sir Paul adopted his first wife Linda Eastman's daughter Heather Louise (born 1962) and, following their marriage, they had three children together. These are Mary Anna (born 1969 and named after Paul's late mother), Stella Nina (born 1971) and his only son James Louis (born 1977 and named after Paul's late father and Linda's later mother Louise).

Rod Stewart

Aged sixty, singer Rod Stewart's seventh child (and third son) by fiancée Penny Lancaster was born on 27 November 2005 and named Alastair Wallace Stewart. Stewart's first child, Sarah Thubron, was born in 1964 to art student Susannah Boffey when he was just nineteen years old. His second daughter, Kimberly, was born in 1979 to first wife Alana Hamilton, with whom he also had first son Sean in 1981. Third daughter Ruby was born in 1987 after a relationship with model Kelly Emberg. Second wife Rachel Hunter bore Stewart's fourth daughter Renee in 1992 and second son Liam in 1994.

Dads Then And Now

As a father, you were once indisputably head of your household. Nowadays you're last in the queue for the bathroom. Fatherhood has changed significantly over the last century. Dads are expected to be more involved with their children, to play an active part in their upbringing and, if you want to remain the family figurehead, you have to keep up with everything that today's independently-minded kids are into.

Then
In 1900, fathers insisted that their children learned to read and write proper English.

Now
Fathers would like it if their children simply spoke some kind of recognizable English.

Then
In 1900, a father's horsepower meant his horses.

Now
It's the size of his minivan.

Then
In 1900, if a father put a roof over his family's head, he was a success.

Now
It takes a roof, pool, stable and four-car garage . . . and that's just the holiday home.

Then

In 1900, a father waited for the doctor to tell him
when the baby arrived.

Now

A father must wear a smock,
know how to breathe and make sure
the digital video camera is fully charged.

Then

In 1900, fathers passed on clothing to their sons.

Now

Kids wouldn't be seen dead wearing your clothes!

Then
In 1900, fathers could count on teaching
their children the family business.

Now
Fathers pray their kids will come home from college
long enough to teach them how to use the computer.

Then
In 1900, a father smoked a pipe
or an after-dinner cigar.

Now
If he tries that, he'll be sent outside
with a lecture on lung cancer.

Then
In 1900, fathers shook their children gently
and whispered, 'Wake up, it's time for school.'

Now
Kids shake their fathers violently at 5.00 a.m. shouting:
'Wake up, it's time for football practice!'

Then
In 1900, a father came home from work to find his wife
and children at the dinner table.

Now
A father comes home to a note: 'Joe's at football,
Carol's at the gym, I'm at yoga, pizza in the fridge.'

Then

In 1900, fathers and sons would have heart-to-heart
conversations while fishing in a stream.

Now

Fathers pluck the headphones
off their sons' ears and shout,
'WHEN YOU HAVE A MINUTE...'

Then

In 1900, if a father had breakfast in bed,
it was eggs, bacon, sausage and fried bread.

Now

Special K, semi-skimmed milk, dry toast
and a lecture on cholesterol.

Then

In 1900, fathers said, 'A man's home is his castle.'

Now

Fathers say, 'Welcome to the money pit.'

Then

In 1900, a happy meal was when Father shared
funny stories around the table.

Now

A Happy Meal is
what Dad buys at McDonald's.

Then
In 1900, when fathers entered the room,
children rose to their feet.

Now
Kids glance up and grunt,
'Dad, you're blocking the TV.'

Then
In 1900, fathers demanded to know
what prospects their daughter's suitors had.

Now
Fathers break the ice by saying,
'So . . . how long have you had your nose piercing?'

Then
In 1900, fathers were never truly appreciated.

Now
In the twenty-first century,
fathers are never truly appreciated.

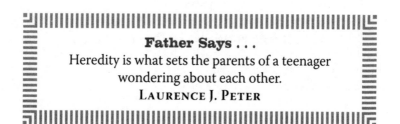

Father Says . . .
Heredity is what sets the parents of a teenager
wondering about each other.
LAURENCE J. PETER

How Father's Day Came to Be

Let's face it, Fathers's Day isn't a patch on Mother's Day. Dads have a long way to go before they catch up on the sort of fuss that is made of mums on Mother's Day. There's no point in complaining about it, though, because that just makes you look ungrateful for the home-made card and the new air freshener for your car. We should remember, too, that Father's Day was invented by a woman, and be suitably thankful.

An American, Sonora Dodd, was the first to have the idea of a Father's Day, dreaming up the idea while listening to a Mother's Day sermon in 1909. Sonora wanted a day to honour her father, William Smart, who was widowed when his wife died giving birth to their sixth child. Mr Smart was left to raise the newborn and his other five children by himself on a farm in eastern Washington state.

The first Father's Day

When Sonora grew up, she realized the selflessness her father had shown in raising his children as a single parent. Sonora's father was born in June, so she chose to hold the first Father's Day celebration in Spokane, Washington on 19 June 1910.

President Calvin Coolidge backed the idea in 1924, but it was 1966 before Lyndon Johnson signed a presidential proclamation declaring the third Sunday of June to be Father's Day. This finally became permanent in 1972.

Roses are the Father's Day flower: red to be worn for a living father and white if the father has died. You have a right to be suspicious, therefore, if you see your wife and kids sharing out white roses on the evening of 18 June!

The First Day at School

The first day of school can be both an exciting *and* stressful occasion for children and parents alike – exciting because it's a milestone event, stressful because it means separation. Whether your child is starting day care, nursery or school, there are many simple things you can do to help prepare them for this new adventure.

Help your child adjust to the feeling of not having you around by leaving them with a relation or friend for a few hours. It will give your child the confidence of knowing that you haven't abandoned them and that you'll be back!

Social skills such as the ability to share, take turns and participate in a group are excellent tools for your child to learn. This makes the child better prepared to deal with new people and situations. Children can start to learn these skills at baby groups or toddler sessions.

Is the new school a good fit for your child? Do *your* homework, go along to open days and, if possible, take your child. Speak to the teachers, ask questions and try to see the school in action.

Is your child's physical development age-appropriate? Children of school age should be able to feed themselves, use the toilet, go up and down stairs and dress themselves. If they are struggling, help them learn for themselves – don't do everything for them.

There are a number of things you can do to help prepare your child for that first-day adventure:

Tell your child in advance to which school they will soon be going. If possible, take a walk to the school so that it becomes familiar.

Be positive and reassure your child that school is a good place. Role-play some enjoyable school activities to which your child can look forward. Preparation is everything: have each item ready before the big day.

Going into class

Many schools allow you to go into class on the first morning to help your child settle. Don't be too concerned if your child cries or refuses to leave your side; teachers are used to this happening. You must let the teacher take charge of your child when the teacher thinks the time is right so that your child can build a trusting relationship. All children take to being left in the teacher's care in different ways and some make more of a fuss for far longer than others. Be assured that the morning routine will quickly become familiar and any associated tantrums will be short-lived.

Try to help your child find a friend! Hopefully your child will be starting school with a familiar face from any pre-school groups you've attended. You should aim to try to go to school together on the big day.

After a few days you will wonder why you were so worried. You will barely merit a second glance as your child bounds into school with their new-found friends!

Dad's Night In

Every so often, you have to let the lady of the house go out for an evening with her girlfriends. It is, after all, the only way you can properly justify your own nights out. This, of course, leaves you in charge of the kids. Try to remember that bit – *you're* in charge, not them. The only way to survive is to plan an effective 'hearts and minds' campaign well in advance. Work out ways to keep them entertained that will also be fun for you. That's the key – make the whole evening fun and you will enjoy yourself, too.

One of the first hurdles you have to clear is feeding time. You can, of course, trawl through the many takeaway menus stuck to the fridge door, but it's much more fun to make a pizza together and watch your favourite movie.

Easy-Bake Oven Pizza

INGREDIENTS:

2¼ tsp milk • 2 tbsp flour
⅛ tsp baking powder
dash salt • 1 tsp margarine
1 tbsp pizza tomato sauce
1½ tbsp shredded mozzarella cheese

1 Preheat the oven for 15 minutes.

2 Slowly adding milk to the mixture, stir together the flour, baking powder, salt and margarine until the dough looks like medium-sized crumbs.

3 Shape the dough into a ball. (Add more flour if it's too sticky.) Put the ball into a greased pan.

④ Use your fingers to pat the dough evenly over the bottom of the pan, then up the sides.

⑤ Pour the pizza tomato sauce evenly over the dough, and then sprinkle with cheese.

⑥ Add toppings of choice.

⑦ Bake for twenty minutes or until golden.

⑧ Slice and enjoy!

Movie time

You don't have to wait until it's Mum's night out. You can make this a special event that involves all the family. Set a movie start time and make sure all chores are complete before the start.

Movies are an escape, so you need the right atmosphere – a darkened room, plenty of comfy seating and movie snacks are a must. If you need to schedule an intermission for bathroom or refreshment breaks, do so to stop unnecessary interruptions – and switch on the answering machine. If there are disagreements about what to watch, write the movie titles on pieces of paper, fold them up and take a lucky dip. If there are still moans and groans, you decide. Remember you *are* supposed to be in charge after all.

Not so long ago, watching a family movie was only possible if you took a trip to the cinema or waited for the inevitable Christmas repeat of *Chitty Chitty Bang Bang* or *The Wizard of Oz*. Nowadays, no sooner has the latest box-office hit finished at the cinema than it's available to rent or buy.

Here are just a few timeless favourites to consider for your 'Dad's Night In'. (Please note: movie ratings should be checked to ensure they are suitable for your child's age group.)

ALL AGES:

Cinderella is based on the world's greatest fairy tale, with its spellbinding story, memorable music, spectacular animation and unforgettable characters.

The Little Mermaid Ariel, a fun-loving and mischievous mermaid, is off on the adventure of a lifetime with her best friend, the adorable Flounder, and the reggae-singing Caribbean crab Sebastian at her side.

Cars is a high-octane animated adventure comedy that shows life is about the journey, not the finish line. Hotshot rookie race car Lightning McQueen is living life in the fast lane until he hits a detour on his way to the most important race of his life.

Shrek is an adaption from William Steig's 1990 fairy tale picture book. The story tells how the ogre, Shrek, is forced by Lord Farquaad to rescue Princess Fiona from a dragon so that Farquaad can marry her. Along the way, Shrek befriends a talking donkey, and falls in love with Fiona. If you like it, look out for *Shrek 2*.

Ice Age This computer-animated film stars friends Sid, the clumsy ground-sloth, and Manfred (Manny), one of the last remaining mammoths. They spot a baby on the bank of the river and decide to return it to its tribe. Follow-up this movie with *Ice Age 2 The Meltdown* for more prehistoric antics.

Finding Nemo This hilarious adventure takes you into the breathtaking underwater world of Australia's Great Barrier Reef. Nemo, an adventurous young clownfish, is unexpectedly taken to a dentist's office aquarium. It's up to Marlin, his worrisome father, and Dory, a friendly but forgetful regal blue tang fish, to make the epic journey to bring Nemo home.

Toy Story was the first full-length computer-animated feature film. Experience a hilarious fantasy about the lives toys lead when they're left alone. Woody, an old-fashioned cowboy doll, is Andy's favourite. But when Andy gets Buzz Lightyear for his birthday, the flashy new space hero takes Andy's room by storm! If you enjoyed going to infinity and beyond, *Toy Story 2* is more of the same.

Madagascar follows the antics of Alex the lion and his best friends Marty the Zebra, Melman the Giraffe and Gloria the Hippo at New York's Central Park Zoo. Along with some hapless penguins the friends escape the zoo only to find themselves being re-captured, darted and crated on a ship for an adventure in Madagascar. These native New Yorkers have to figure out how to survive in the wild and experience the true meaning of the phrase 'It's a jungle out there.'

Monsters Inc. This visually dazzling, action-packed animation stars James P. Sullivan (Sulley) and his wisecracking best friend, Mike Wazowski. They work at Monsters, Inc., the largest scream-processing factory in Monstropolis. Monsters believe children are dangerous and toxic, however, and they are scared silly when a little girl wanders into their world. Sulley and Mike face monstrous intrigue and some hilarious misadventures along the way.

The Lion King follows the adventures of Simba, the feisty lion cub who 'just can't wait to be king.' But his envious Uncle Scar has plans for his own ascent to the throne, and he forces Simba's exile from the kingdom. Alone and adrift, Simba soon joins the escapades of a hilarious meerkat named Timon and his warmhearted warthog pal, Pumbaa. Adopting their carefree lifestyle, Simba ignores his real responsibilities until he realizes his destiny and returns to claim his place in the 'Circle of Life.'

FOR AGES 10 YEARS PLUS:

Spy Kids is bursting with an awesome array of ultra-cool, high-tech gadgetry. This first movie introduces top international spies Gregorio and Ingrid Cortez who traded the excitement of espionage for the adventure of parenthood. But when they're called out on a secret mission, the Cortezes are separated from their family and kidnapped by the evil Fegan Floop. Children Carmen and Juni bravely crisscross the globe in a thrilling quest to save their parents.

Charlie And The Chocolate Factory is adapted from Roald Dahl's classic story about eccentric chocolatier Willy Wonka and Charlie, a boy from a poor family who lives in the shadow of Wonka's extraordinary factory. Wonka launches a worldwide contest to select an heir to his candy empire. Five lucky children, including Charlie, draw golden tickets from Wonka chocolate bars and win a guided tour of the legendary candy-making facility that no outsider has seen in fifteen years.

FOR 12 YEARS PLUS:

The Chronicles Of Narnia: The Lion, The Witch And The Wardrobe A feature-length film from the classic story by C.S. Lewis stars Lucy, Edmund, Susan, and Peter, four siblings who find the world of Narnia through a magical wardrobe while playing a game of 'hide-and-seek' at the country estate of a mysterious professor. Follow the children as they lead Narnia into a spectacular climactic battle.

Harry Potter and the Philosopher's Stone The first adaptation from J K Rowling's series of novels about a seemingly ordinary eleven-year-old boy who is actually a wizard and survivor of an attempted murder by the evil Lord Voldemort. If this debut film leaves you spellbound, make a date with its sequels for further adventures with Harry and friends.

Star Wars Take your pick from the 2005 release of *Revenge of the Sith* to the first *Star Wars* of 1977. With a total of six titles to choose from, the saga is a must for all science fiction fans.

Spiderman 1 and *2* bring the Marvel Comic superhero character to life in two action packed films. Follow Peter Parker/Spiderman battling with the Green Goblin and Doctor Octopus in these dramatic blockbusters.

King Kong is the all-action 2006 remake of the original 1933 King Kong film about a fictional giant ape called Kong who is discovered living in a massive jungle where prehistoric creatures have been protected and hidden for millions of years. Make yourself comfortable for this feature-length three-hours-and-eight-minute adventure.

Pirates Of The Caribbean – The Curse Of The Black Pearl follows roguish yet charming pirate captain Jack Sparrow, played unforgettably by Johnny Depp. Rich in suspense-filled adventure, sword-clashing action, mystery, humour and unforgettable characters, it's an all-round winner – and don't miss the 2006 sequel, *Dead Man's Chest*.

Ten Ways to Get
Some Peace and Quiet

1. Get your parents/family to take the children out. On an outing, that is, not like a sniper would.

2. Buy all your kids headphones for the TV/DVD/CD player and make sure the things will work for their computer games, too.

3. Lock yourself in the cupboard under the stairs.

4. Convert your basement into a mini theme park.

5. Kit your garden shed out with a PlayStation/TV and/or stereo just for you – remember to buy a padlock.

6. Treat your partner each time it's her birthday (or yours) to a night away at a hotel and get your family to move in and look after the children. Remember to go home again.

7. Install an outside toilet where you can disappear with the Sunday papers.

8. Keep up your hobbies – your partner won't deny you time doing these and it will give you the perfect excuse for time on your own. If your favourite hobby is climbing Mount Everest, so much the better.

9. Buy a one-man tent, put it up in the back garden and pretend you are trekking across Antarctica. Remember to do this in wintertime, only so that there is little likelihood that the rest of the family will want to come, too.

10. Buy a second home that needs work and excuse yourself at weekends while you go over to do some work on it. Remember to take a newspaper/books and a crate of beer. Forget to take your mobile phone.

Things You'll Never Hear
a Dad Say

◆ Well, how about that? I'm lost! Looks like we'll have to stop and ask for directions.

◆ Here's the keys to my new car – GO CRAZY!

◆ What do you mean you wanna play football? Is ballet not good enough for you, son?

◆ Your mother and I are going away for the weekend. Have some friends over – better still, have a party!

◆ I don't know what's wrong with your car. Just have it towed to a mechanic and pay whatever he asks.

◆ No son of mine is going to live under this roof without a tattoo. Now quit whining and let's go get you one!

◆ What do you want a job for? I make plenty of money for you to spend.

◆ I don't think age matters in a relationship – after all, he's only fifteen years older than you.

◆ Here's my PIN number and credit card.

◆ Of course you can go to an all-night party – ring me at 4.00 a.m. and I'll collect you.

◆ Father's Day? Don't worry about that – it's no big deal.

How to Teach Your Child to Ride a Bike

Remember learning to ride your first two-wheeled bike without trainer wheels? Remember how scared you were? Remember how your dad giggled? Now it's your turn.

Learning to ride a two-wheeler is an important milestone in any child's life and as a Dad you won't want to miss it. It's not all fun, though. You'll be the one trotting along beside the bike for miles with your back bent at a hideously unnatural and painful angle so that you can reach down to steady the bike by gripping the back of the saddle while every turn of the pedals scrapes another layer of skin off of your shin. Why on earth would you want to miss that?

Preparation

◆ Make sure the bike is the right size for your child.

◆ Install training wheels if not already fitted.

◆ Buy a suitably-sized helmet and make sure your child wears it every time they ride.

◆ Consider knee and elbow pads, as well.

◆ Be sure clothing worn is protective and not so loose that it will get caught up in the bike.

◆ Explain the importance of biking in safe locations and of wearing protective clothing.

◆ Discuss what to do if they fall, and explain that this is part of the learning process.

◆ Establish a safe and local learning place. A field with short, hard-packed grass or a path surrounded by grass would be ideal. There should be plenty of open space, flat ground and no traffic.

Biking

◆ Get your child onto the bike and pedaling, with you walking alongside them.

◆ Ask them to think about balancing on the wheels of the bike alone. Explain that eventually you will take the training wheels off.

◆ Let your child ride the bike as often as possible with the training wheels. Be sure they learn how to stop effectively.

Trainers off

◆ Only remove the training wheels when your child is totally comfortable riding the bike.

◆ Take hold of bike and child – the seat of the bike and the back of the child's sweatshirt, or one handlebar and the sweatshirt.

◆ Push and run along with the child, instructing them to keep pedaling and to look straight ahead.

◆ Take your hand off the seat when you feel the child balancing on their own.

◆ Encourage them as you take your hand from the child's sweatshirt.

◆ Repeat the previous three steps until the child is able to start pedaling without you.

There may be a few crashes and tumbles, but children are remarkably resilient and with a few words of comfort and a cuddle, your youngster will get back on the bike. They all want to be able to ride like the older kids. They may need a couple of sessions but, once your child has mastered the art of pedaling and balancing, he or she will progress very quickly.

You have a right to feel proud, but there's also a hint of sadness when you see them cycling off on their own. It's one more little thing that they no longer need you for!

Getting the Kids to Bed on Time

When there's something you want to watch on TV, or you have some friends round for dinner, getting the kids to bed can be a nightmare. They don't like to be left out. Putting them to bed, and persuading them to stay there, can involve using up all your best bribes and threats. The best way to tackle it is to make sure that they are good and ready for bed.

You need to have a routine. Children know where they are with a familiar routine. Some people are more organized than others by nature, but anyone can put routines and systems in place that will help maintain a happy atmosphere at the end of the day.

End of the school holidays
It may be difficult at first to get children back on schedule, so start introducing the regular bedtime a few days before the school term.

Exercise
School may be a mental challenge but they certainly won't be physically exhausted. Make sure they have plenty of fresh air and exercise. Walk to and from school rather than taking the car. Walk the dog, play in the park, go swimming or sign them up for after-school sports clubs. If children don't expend energy during the day, they are likely to have trouble falling asleep at night.

Homework
Don't leave homework until late in the evening. If there are a number of tasks to be completed, put these in order of importance and ensure all materials, reference books or whatever else is needed are at hand before starting. Make sure there are no distractions and have a regular quiet study area.

Prepare for the day ahead

Before bedtime, have all items ready for the next day. A clear mind will ensure trouble-free sleep. Keep a 'to-do' list as a reminder of what things are needed for different classes. Homework assignments, PE kits or musical instruments can be ticked off when laid out and ready.

Meal time

Try to have a family meal together at a reasonable time. Use the time to chat about your day and theirs. Avoid stimulants such as fizzy drinks, chocolate or sweets.

Wind down

Once the work and chores of the day are completed, have some fun – it can't be all work and no play. Let them have some free time to wind down and do what they want to do. After all, they are children . . .

Routine

The number-one way to eliminate bedtime battles is to establish a ritual and stick with it no matter what. Even though they may object at first, they will get used to it.

Relaxation

A nightly warm bath slows the heart rate, relaxes muscles and aids a restful night's sleep. Bath time can be fun, too, but don't let the bubble fights or naval battles drag on too long.

Quiet time

Nearly there! Choose a favourite story book, get them tucked up in bed and read away. If they are of an age to read themselves, involve them by reading a page each in turn. You might also give them time to read for ten minutes before lights out.

Goodnight and sweet dreams. Now what was it you wanted to watch on TV . . .?

Top Tips for a Stress-Free Morning

With time at a premium, a queue for the bathroom and bears with sore heads everywhere, canny Dads need to have a strategy to survive early-morning madness.

Don't always blame the children for the way you feel every morning. If you feel grumpy and stressed this will rub off on the children and make them feel resentful and grumpy, too.

A non-negotiable routine is a requirement, not an option. It must be established with the consequences discussed and determined. For instance, if you don't get up at the first time of asking, bedtime will be fifteen minutes earlier tonight.

A.M. essentials

Although these require planning, they often save time in the long run and avoid battles and disagreements.

1. Have a running order for the bathroom and make it clear that if you snooze, you lose!

2. Have all uniform/clothes laid out ready. Doing this the night before is a good idea.

3. Don't be caught out during the onset of different seasons. When the summer heatwave hits unexpectedly in May, have in-date sunscreen and sunhats ready.

4. At the start of autumn don't wait for the first frost to find that missing glove in the understairs cupboard. Plan ahead and have clothing, shoes, hats and scarves ready.

5 Make sure PE kits, special items or requirements for lessons are ready. The last thing you need is to be asked for ingredients for a cake at 7.00 a.m. in the morning.

6 Ensure schoolbags are packed with any necessary homework. Nothing's worse than remembering the homework is on the kitchen table when you're halfway to school.

7 Breakfast is important. Many experts argue that it is the *most* important meal of the day, so your kids need a nutritious start. Decide on breakfast choices and even set the table to gather everyone together.

8 Prepare and refrigerate packed lunches the previous night.

9 Why not have 10–15 minutes to yourself to have a relaxing shower and cup of tea or a little exercise routine before the children wake?

10 If your children do not wake by themselves, try playing some soft music or an audio story ten minutes before they need to get up.

Remember to talk, too. Chat about the fun things you can do together after school or at the weekend. You need to keep things positive and happy for a good start to the day. And above all, keep smiling!

Pocket Money – What It Will Cost You!

Just accept it – you are the family banker. You don't get to charge interest or call in loans; your banking system is more of a one-way cash flow with none of it trickling in your direction. As your children grow older, you'll find you have more to do and your free time will quickly disappear. You will have to make time for running them round to their friends' houses, taking them to after-school activities like football, ballet or music lessons and helping them with their (more-complicated-by-the-year) homework.

To give yourself time to do these things, it's vital that you get the kids 'trained' at an early age to help around the house, and the best way to do that is bribery! You can't call it anything else, because if it weren't for the monetary reward the odds are that they simply wouldn't do it.

You can start them off with little jobs like tidying up the toys in their room and putting their dirty clothes in the wash basket. Once they get that little bit older, they can help their younger siblings get dressed and clean their teeth. When they can be trusted not to break things, they can progress to washing the dishes and making their own sandwiches and by the time they approach their teenage years they'll be keen to cut the grass or wash the car.

Older and wiser

Of course, the older they get and the more complex household chores they tackle, the greater the financial reward they will expect. Whereas you were paying your eight- year-old fifty pence a week to do several sinks full of dishes, your twelve-year-old will realize that taking your car to the carwash costs you around a fiver, so they will expect a fee closer to this for performing the task on you driveway.

Whatever the financial damage to your wallet, it's worth getting the children to help out because it allows you some time to put your feet up or to do something that you enjoy – providing that they've left you with some pocket money, too!

Father Says . . .
Telling a teenager the facts of life
is like giving a fish a bath.
ARNOLD H. GLASOW

Fatherhood – the Balance Sheet

Pocket money might become a bit of a drain on your cash resources, but it's really the least of your financial problems when it comes to raising kids. Children are expensive and have an annoying habit of outgrowing clothes and shoes faster than you can say 'overdraft'. Some of the financial burden involved with children, however, sneak past you almost unnoticed.

Before the birth

Everyone knows that bringing up a child is an expensive business. But did you know that parents spend an average of £1,560 on their baby – before it's even born? In a survey carried out in the UK, eight out of ten parents said they start spending on the new addition to their family before they are six months into the pregnancy.

The average parents-to-be spend £1,060 on essentials for their baby, such as prams, car seats, changing and feeding equipment, baby monitors, toys and clothes.

Women spend a further £500 each on maternity wear, books, magazines and even pampering treatments and health supplements during their pregnancy.

Nearly eighty per cent of parents pay out to redecorate a room as a nursery, while twenty per cent go so far as moving house, at an estimated cost of around £4,250 (not counting extra mortgage payments or taxes).

One in seven said they spent between £2,000 and £2,500 getting ready for their new baby, while two per cent claimed to spend more than £5,800.

Apparently the biggest wastes of money were said to be baby carriers, followed by bottle warmers.

Growing pains and prices

According to new research, raising a child now costs more than the average UK house. From birth to leaving university at age twenty-one it costs parents £140,398 to feed, clothe and school their children. This compares to the £137,800 cost of an average home.

The total cost of raising a child is more than twice the national average household's take-home pay, meaning workers in the average family will spend at least two years working to cover the cost of each child.

Looking regionally across the UK, there's an apparent North-South divide in the cost involved; Dads in London (£163,322), the South-East (£156,087) and East Anglia (£148,406) spend the most on raising their children, while Dads spending the least are in Yorkshire & Humberside (£127,463), followed by the North-East (£131,240) and the West Midlands (£133,916).

Fathers in Britain spend significantly more on raising their offspring than their European counterparts – some thirty per cent more than parents in France.

Babies may be high maintenance but are relatively cheap to run, costing around £40 a week in their first year of life. However, the average 16-year-old costs £64 a week with some £22 going on food, £14 a week on entertainment and after-school activities, £9 a week on pocket money and £7 a week on clothes.

For private schooling the average day pupil fee is nearly £8,000 per school year.

One of the biggest child-related expenses after private schooling is holidays, costing around £700.

But the little darlings are worth every penny, aren't they . . . *aren't* they?

A Dads' Guide to the Internet

Even the greatest Luddites among us have, by now, been forced to accept that computers are now part of our daily lives. Most of us use email every day at work and when the system crashes, we all look blank, or curse, or throw our hands in the air. A kid who looks no older than the one you packed off to school that morning eventually shows up to fix it all.

You have to accept that your children's computer skills will soon far outstrip any that you may have acquired yourself but, whatever your age, the fact that you are – or soon will be – a father means that you will have to try to keep up.

Home computing surged in the 1980s as prices of machines like the Spectrum ZX-81 and the Commodore 64 plummeted, making them affordable to the average family.

Nowadays, your child will have access to computers at school, and households without computers are few and far between. You can buy an Internet-ready computer for less than £500 from many high-street retailers. But it's not only youngsters who become addicted to the Internet; pensioners have also joined the revolution and been labelled the Silver Surfers!

Birth of the Internet

The Internet began in the 1960s as a US Department of Defense communication network but university researchers and professors started using it to communicate with others in their fields. Internet use exploded in the early 1990s with the arrival of the World Wide Web which made it easier to find and view information online. No one – no single country, organization, or company – is in charge of the Internet.

That means that parents need to take responsibility for the pages that their children are viewing. Most computers can be set up with parental controls, so make sure they're set before you allow your child to go online. If you have any problems setting your computer up, don't be afraid to ask for help. You can pay a professional to do this, but if you ask around you are more than likely to find you have a friend or colleague who would willingly give up some of their time to help. Just don't ask your kids to set up the parental control because then they'll then know how to turn it off!

Here are some basic tips for surfing the net safely:

1. It is best to keep the computer in a family or shared room so that your teenager isn't shut away in their bedroom for hours without supervision.

2. Talk to your children about Internet safety. There are unscrupulous people online who use the Internet as a tool to further their seedy obsessions. Let your child know that it's OK to tell you if they have come across anything that is worrying them.

3. Help your children set up their email accounts and 'spam' filters.

4. Limit the amount of unsupervised time your children spend online.

5. Several charities like the NCH and Barnados are members of the Children's Charities' Coalition for Internet Safety (CHIS). Don't be afraid to do some research on how to make your child's online time safer while still allowing them their independence.

Surfing the Internet together can be fun for homework projects or when looking at holiday destinations and, if you're not already into online games or regular computer games, try having a go. You may find it just as addictive as your kids do, so be prepared to limit your time on the computer, too!

Are We There Yet?

There's nothing worse than setting out on a long car journey with the kids in the back seat all moaning about being bored. They will be hugely entertained with the grown-ups in the front seats start arguing about exactly where they should have turned off the motorway and whose fault it is that you are now all hopelessly lost . . . and beware the child who has learned to mimic the sound of your sat nav's voice! Keeping the kids entertained on a long trip, however, should be more involving and more fun than simply sticking a portable DVD player in front of them.

Why not make the car journey an enjoyable part of the journey? Try playing your music to your kids and getting them to like it – otherwise you run the risk of spending two hours listening to Eminem or Girls Aloud or, if you're very unlucky, both.

If your music really doesn't appeal, try some audio books. You could also try investing in portable CD or MP3 players so that everyone gets to listen to what they like without squabbling over whose turn it is to have Will Young blasting out.

Failing all this, you can try the traditional musical route. Swallow hard, breathe deeply and prepare yourself for that gruelling drive while you sing the following (repeatedly):

The Wheels On The Bus

The wheels on the bus go round and round
Round and round, round and round
The wheels on the bus go round and round
All day long

The wipers on the bus go 'Swish, swish, swish,
Swish, swish, swish, swish, swish, swish'
The wipers on the bus go 'Swish, swish, swish'
All day long

The horn on the bus goes 'Beep, beep, beep
Beep, beep, beep, beep, beep, beep'
The horn on the bus goes 'Beep, beep, beep'
All day long

The baby on the bus goes, 'Wah, wah, wah!
Wah, wah, wah, wah, wah, wah!'
The baby on the bus goes, 'Wah, wah, wah!'
All day long

The people on the bus say, 'Shh, shh, shh,
Shh, shh, shh, shh, shh, shh'
The people on the bus say, 'Shh, shh, shh'
All day long.

You may also find that a child's version of the variety of bus passengers includes dogs, cats, cows and elephants, with the bus inevitably heading towards 'Old MacDonald's Farm'.

She'll Be Coming Round The Mountain

She'll be coming round the mountain
When she comes
She'll be coming round the mountain
When she comes
She'll be coming round the mountain,
She'll be coming round the mountain,
She'll be coming round the mountain
When she comes

She'll be driving six white horses
When she comes
(Yee ha!)
She'll be driving six white horses
When she comes
(Yee ha!)
She'll be driving six white horses,
She'll be driving six white horses,
She'll be driving six white horses
When she comes
(Yee ha!)

Oh, we'll all go out to meet her
When she comes
Oh, we'll all go out to meet her
When she comes
Oh, we'll all go out to meet her,
We'll all go out to meet her,
We'll all go out to meet her
When she comes

She'll be wearing red pyjamas
When she comes

She'll be wearing red pyjamas
When she comes
She'll be wearing red pyjamas,
She'll be wearing red pyjamas,
She'll be wearing red pyjamas
When she comes

Other possibilities include:

Songs from musicals:
The Sound of Music,
Chitty Chitty Bang Bang,
Mary Poppins, etc.

'Hush-a-bye Baby'

'Lavender's Blue'

'London Bridge'

'Oranges and Lemons'

'The Grand Old Duke of York'

'This Old Man'

'Frère Jacques'

Anything by the Beatles,
ABBA or the Beach Boys

Action songs are always hilarious in the car – remember not to join in if you are the driver – and often cause passengers of overtaking vehicles to peer in wondering what you are doing as you wave your hands frantically while nodding your head and attempting to stamp your feet.

So, it's time to go. You're in the car, you start the ignition, everyone's strapped in, all together now: 'The wheels on the bus go round and round . . .'

How to Make a Kite

There's no way that you'll be able to tackle this without humming 'Let's Go Fly A Kite' from *Mary Poppins*, so don't even attempt it – just let the music take you! If you've never watched Mary Poppins with your kids, then get it on DVD and find out how one hopeless dad thrills his kids by patching up an old kite.

You don't have to patch up a kite, you can make your own just by following these simple instructions, and maybe impressing the kids with your encyclopedic knowledge of kites and kite-making.

Stories to impress the kids

Some of the earliest known kites came from the South Sea Islands where natives used them to fish, attaching bait to the tail of the kite and a net to catch the fish. Even today, kites are used as a fishing aid in the Solomon Islands in the Pacific Ocean. In the Polynesian Islands, kites were associated with gods. A kite represented the god Tane and the Maori god Rehua is depicted as a bird. Rehuna is thought to be the ancestor of all kites.

China is widely accepted as the actual birthplace of kites. One story tells of a general, Huan Theng, who, in the year 202 BC, was inspired when his hat was blown from his head. The general flew kites made of thin pieces of bamboo that hummed and shrieked in the wind over an enemy encampment at night. The opposing army ran away, believing they were plagued by evil spirits out to destroy them. Both the Chinese and the Japanese learned to use huge kites to raise soldiers into the air to spy on enemy positions. Old prints show warriors flying over enemy territory.

Technical terms

A simple kite is made from the following basic components:

1 The spine – the vertical stick you build your kite around.

2 The spar – the support stick(s), placed crossways or at a slant over the spine.

3 The frame – joining spine and spars, this forms the shape of the kite and makes a support for the cover.

4 The sail – the paper, plastic or cloth that covers the frame.

5 The bridle – one or more strings attached to the spine or spars which helps control the kite in the air.

6 The flying line – the string running from the bridle which you hold to fly the kite.

7 The tail – a long strip of paper or plastic or ribbon that helps balance the kite in flight. Not all kites need tails.

To make a diamond-shaped kite you will need

◆ Thin garden twine

◆ Scotch tape or glue

◆ 1 sheet of strong paper (102 cm × 102 cm)

◆ 2 strong, straight wooden sticks of bamboo or wooden dowelling 90 cm and 100 cm

◆ Markers, paint or crayons to decorate your kite.

◆ Scissors

1. Make a cross with the two sticks, the shorter stick (spar) placed horizontally across the longer stick (spine). Make sure that both sides of the spar are equal in width.

2. Tie the two sticks together with string, making sure they are at right angles to each other. A dab of glue can be used to secure them in place.

3. Cut a notch at each end of the spine and spar deep enough to hold the type of string you are using. Cut a piece of string long enough to stretch all around the kite frame. Make a small loop in the string and lay this through the top notch, then tie the string round the spine below the notch. Wrapping the string around the top of the spine a couple of times will help to fasten it tightly.

4. Stretch the string down through the notch at one end of the spar. Then stretch it on down to the bottom of the spine, fastening it as you did at the top, laying another small loop through the bottom notch.

5. Next stretch the string up through the notch at the other end of the spar and back to the top of the spine where you need to tie it off tightly, wrapping it

round the spine again a couple of times, and cut off any string you don't need. This string frame must be taut, but not so tight as to warp the sticks.

6 Lay the sail material flat and place the stick frame face down on top. Cut around it, leaving about 2–3 cm for a margin. Fold these edges over the string frame and tape or glue it down so that the material is tight.

7 Cut a piece of string about 120 cm long, and tie one end to the loop at the top of the spine and the other end to the loop at the bottom. Tie another small loop in the string just above the intersection of the two crosspieces. This will be the kite's bridle, the string to which the flying line is attached.

8 Make a tail by tying a small ribbon roughly every 10 cm along the length of string. Attach the tail to the loop at the bottom of the kite.

9 Decorate!

Top tips

◆ Cut *away* from you! It is safer and gives you far better control of the scissors or a knife.

◆ Spray-can glue is really good for patching up paper kites.

◆ Stability is improved by the use of a bow tied as part of a flexible tail.

◆ Hold your kite up by the string when you are finished to see if it is balanced. You can balance it by glueing more paper on the lighter side.

◆ Kites are different each time you make one, so slight adjustments might need to be made for each kite.

Safety

◆ Never fly kites near airfields, overhead power lines, roads and railways.

◆ Do not fly kites in thunderstorms.

◆ Avoid flying over the heads of people or animals.

◆ The legal UK flight limit is 60 m (200 ft).

◆ Wear protective gloves, especially for larger kites in strong winds.

◆ Avoid other kites.

◆ Wear good sunglasses if you are looking up a lot on a sunny day.

In the Garden with Dad

If you enjoy gardening, the last thing you need is a 'little helper' trampling your flower beds and ripping out seedlings instead of weeds. You can't, however, exclude the kids from the garden when you are out there. On the other hand, if you think of gardening as a huge chore, interference from the kids will only stop you from getting it all over and done with. In either case, what you need to do is spend a little time on garden pursuits with the kids to keep them out from under your feet.

Children are fascinated by all of the things that you would rather not see in your garden. Spiders and flies, ladybugs and aphids, slugs and snails, woodlice and ants – kids just love them. Bug hunting is one way of occupying their time while you get on with the gardening. If you're not already an expert on creepy-crawlies, do some background research because kids will always ask questions when you go bug hunting together.

Bug box
Buy or make a bug box, which is usually a plastic cube with a magnifier built into the lid. Anything placed inside the box is magnified through the lid. The small size allows it to be easily carried in your pocket and is just the ticket for viewing bugs, rocks or plant material.

Start by looking in your own garden: some creatures live behind bushes or among flowers and grass, while others crawl beneath rocks, burrow underground, or swim in ponds. You can check what should be around at certain times of the year by looking things up on the Internet or visiting your local library. You can then set yourself and your child a few tasks, such as:

◆ Identify the most common insects local to your home.

◆ Identify the characteristics of the insect.

◆ Describe the process of metamorphosis of a caterpillar to a butterfly.

◆ Identify the various roles of bees such as queen, workers, etc. in making honey.

◆ Identify the parts of an ant's anatomy and the roles within an ant colony.

Ground force

There are few things children enjoy more than digging in the dirt and making mud pies, but they also enjoy planting seeds, watching them grow and harvesting what they have grown. This helps them to learn that potatoes and carrots come from the earth – not from the supermarket.

Encourage their enthusiasm by planting seeds that mature quickly and are large enough for a child to handle easily. Sunflower seeds can produce spectacular results.

Vegetables are a good choice for young children. They germinate quickly and can be eaten when mature. Children may even be motivated to eat vegetables that they have grown themselves even when they would normally turn their noses up at them.

To add interest and colour to the vegetable garden, you might want to add some flowers such as marigolds or sweet peas. Be sure any flowers you plant are non-toxic.

If you don't have a garden, try using pots or containers on a window sill. Herbs are a good choice to plant indoors for children as they grow fast and can then be tasted. Or try a packet of cress seeds on some damp kitchen towel, which will quickly produce a crop of cress ready for use in a sandwich.

If your child appears to be developing green fingers, when it comes to their birthday or Christmas, why not buy them kid-sized garden tools such as a rake, shovel or fork – or maybe their very own wheelbarrow?

During the winter months, try keeping the children busy by planting pots with spring flower bulbs, ideal as Christmas gifts for relations or teachers. Plant the pots with crocuses, narcissi or hyacinths, as forcing flower bulbs is an easy and inexpensive project with spectacular results in the spring.

Most children enjoy Halloween and having a pumpkin lit on the doorstep. Growing your own in the garden needs a fair amount of space, so it might be better to make a visit to a local farm shop. Children will be amazed at the many varieties available, the different sizes and how they grow.

During the summer months, collect flower petals and leaves for pressing. Either press between blotting paper inside a heavy book or purchase a small flower press. Your child can enjoy hours of fun creating handmade gifts such as cards, bookmarks or pictures for family and friends.

Garden games

There are lots of fun games to be played in the garden, some of which don't need much space. Introduce your child to garden bowls, croquet, pitch and putt, skittles or quoits for hours of family fun on a summer's afternoon. You can buy these or make your own.

Feathered friends

Another way of making the most of your garden is by encouraging birds to nest and feed. If you haven't got a bird book on your bookshelf, visit your local library for more information. Begin by identifying the birds and for a closer look use a pair

of binoculars. Make lists of the
different species that visit your
garden and in a timescale of, say,
ten minutes count the number
of different birds that appear.

Keep your garden birds fed by
making a simple bird feeder. This is
what you will need to do:

1 **Modify a yoghurt pot**
Carefully make a small hole in the bottom. Thread
string through the hole and tie a knot on the inside.
Leave enough string so that you can tie the pot to a tree
or your bird table.

2 **Prepare some lard**
Allow some lard to warm up to room temperature, but
don't melt it. Once it's warm, cut it up into small pieces
and put it in the mixing bowl.

3 **Add the tasty treats**
Add birdseed, raisins and grated cheese to the soft lard
and mix together. Keep adding the dry mixture until
the fat holds it all together.

4 **Chill the 'cakes'**
Fill your yoghurt pots with bird 'cake' mixture and put
them in the fridge for an hour or so to set.

5 **Add the finishing touch**
Carefully cut away most of the sides of the yoghurt pot
without disturbing the hardened 'cake' inside. You
should leave the base and part of the sides. Then hang
your bird cakes from trees or your bird table.

Ten Top Computer Games

Here are the hottest games on screen at the present moment. Buy or rent one of these and be your kids' hero for ever!

1 *FIFA 07* (PS2)

2 *The Sims 2: Pets* (PC DVD)

3 *New Super Mario Bros* (Nintendo DS)

4 *Gears of War* (Xbox 360)

5 *Animal Crossing: Wild World* (Nintendo DS)

6 *Need for Speed: Carbon* (PS2)

7 *Pro Evolution Soccer 6* (PS2)

8 *Lego Star Wars II: The Original Trilogy* (PS2)

9 *Grand Theft Auto: Vice City Stories* (PSP)

10 *The Legend of Zelda: Twilight Princess* (Wii)

Family Pets

Just because your kids went all gooey-eyed when they saw a puppy in the park, doesn't mean you should rush out and buy them one, no matter how much they pester you. Pets can teach children responsibility and provide love and companionship, but there are many questions to ask yourself – and them – before you add a pet to your family.

Are you willing to take on the added responsibility?

Before you ask whether your child is ready, you should start by asking if YOU are ready for a pet. The ultimate responsibility for a pet is in your hands. A pet is likely to make changes in your life. Some pets are almost as disruptive as a new baby, waking you at night and damaging things in your home.

When is the right time?

Just because the neighbour's dog had the most adorable puppies does not mean you should get one. Consider the decision carefully. It's probably not the right time to get a new pet if you have a child in the house who is under the age of two, you are planning to move, or a holiday is around the corner. Put at least a month's thought into the decision.

Is your child ready?

Children as young as three can help care for a pet, with your supervision.

- ◆ They can play gently with the pet.

- ◆ They can give the pet treats.

- ◆ They can fill food and water dishes.

◆ They can brush and groom cats and dogs.

◆ They can give love, attention and respect.

Even though young children can be involved in pet care, they aren't ready to take over fully until their teenage years. Adults need to oversee the job to make sure that the child does what is necessary to take care of the animal properly. Animals should not suffer neglect because children are only beginning to learn responsibility.

A few things to teach your child about animals

◆ Never touch an animal's food.

◆ Wash hands after touching an animal.

◆ Let an adult clean up animal waste.

◆ Avoid teasing or provoking an animal.

◆ Pay attention to ways an animal tells you it doesn't like what you are doing. Help your child 'listen' to the animal.

Keeping pets is an educational, fun way to introduce kids to responsibilities. The key to a successful pairing lies in choosing the appropriate pet for your child's abilities, age and interests, as well as what you're willing to tolerate in the house.

Wait until your child expresses an interest in getting a pet. If you bring something home for them before they mention it, there's a very good chance that they'll be disinterested, and you've just given yourself a new pet to care for.

Discuss the animal in question with your child. If you're not willing to have certain animals around, make sure you provide some alternative suggestions.

Research the different possibilities together with your child. Libraries have hundreds of animal care books, or browse the pet section at a book store.

Read up on whichever pet you both decide on *before* you buy it. There may be elements of its care and feeding that you weren't initially aware of which make the difference between it being suitable or unsuitable.

If possible, buy the equipment such as a bed, cage, litter tray and toys a day or so before you get your pet.

Warnings

Your child may lose interest in whatever animal you choose, no matter how enthusiastic they were at the beginning. If you're not willing to become the animal's carer should this happen, you should not be considering bringing a pet into the household. If circumstances conspire to make it impossible for you to keep a pet you have bought, make arrangements well in advance with a school or friend who will adopt it.

Consider vets' fees and boarding arrangements when on holiday. These may be worth pricing before purchasing a pet.

If your goal in giving your children a pet is to teach children responsibility, make sure you are being responsible yourself. Finding a new home for an animal or taking it to a shelter when the kids lose interest only teaches them that responsibilities can be abandoned once you decide you're bored. If the whole family is not willing to make sure the new animal is cared for throughout its lifetime, get your child a plant or a virtual pet instead.

Low Maintenance Pets

Taking your child's dog for a walk last thing at night when it's freezing cold and raining is nobody's idea of fun. Neither is waking up thinking you're having a heart attack, with a strange tightness in your chest and a feeling of breathlessness, only to find the cat sitting on you.

If your offspring want a pet, but you don't think the novelty will take long to wear off, or you're not too keen on animals yourself, here are a few suggestions for pets that require the minimum of maintenance.

Pet rocks
Back in 1975, American businessman Gary Dahl came up with this great idea and for a while it was the biggest fad. Here was a pet that took no care and gave its owner a few moments of pleasure. They were, however, easily lost if you let them out in the garden and didn't really return any affection lavished upon them. They were as good as a guard dog for protecting your home, though, because you could throw them at a burglar.

Stick insects
They might not do much, but stick insects are a fascinating low-maintenance pet. There are over 3,000 species and they all feed exclusively on vegetation. Almost all captive stick insects will eat bramble blackberry leaves. They are relatively easy to handle, but you have to be careful with them; cages should be at the right temperature and humidity (as close to the wild as possible) and size; the insects need to be able to hang on to the vegetation to feed and live.

Worms
You don't even need a garden for this, as wormeries are available through various retail outlets. They are compact and will

sit in a corner of your abode, are simple to put together and when the inhabitants arrive, you can feed them your organic kitchen waste.

Goldfish

Fish are one of the easiest animals to keep as pets. They require little looking after, though they need a proper tank to give them enough oxygen (traditional goldfish bowls don't provide this). They should be fed every couple of days with specially prepared food and their water should be changed every week or so. To keep their home fresh and clean, plants can be added to the aquarium tank and a filter is a good idea.

Frogspawn

You'll need a garden for this, and check that you don't harvest the spawn from a protected area as frogs are declining in the wild. Find some spawn, leave it in your own pond in the back garden and it'll eventually hatch into tadpoles, which will turn into froglets. Frogs are great friends of the gardener, feeding on all manner of unwanted insects and pests – and as wild creatures they take no looking after. Just provide them with some stones for shelter and some plant cover.

Tortoises

Though rapidly disappearing from their countries of origin, tortoises are still available and make good, easy pets – but you do need a garden that's secure and has plenty of cover as they like to roam. They need regular water and food like lettuce, tomatoes, dandelion leaves and other fruit and veg. When autumn comes, place them in a wooden box with plenty of straw in a shed or garage where they will be protected from the cold. Your tortoise will hibernate till the spring as they are cold-blooded reptiles and cannot survive harsh cold spells.

Snakes

They may not be everybody's idea of a fun pet, but snakes are relatively easy to look after – they need warmth and a safe place to live like an aquarium-type tank. The only problem is that they like live food such as insects (grasshoppers) or mice, but they do sleep a lot once they've been fed.

Hamsters

One of the cutest pets, hamsters are rodents like mice and guinea pigs. They don't require a huge amount of looking after, but they do need a nice spacious cage with some activities and need to be regularly watered and fed. Buy nuts and seeds for them from the local pet store. They also need to be cleaned out twice a week. Regular handling usually makes hamsters tame and friendly.

Rabbits

Unlike rodents, rabbits are not for flats and town houses. Ideally they need a hutch and a run in a garden for optimum quality of life. They are also easy to handle and one of the most popular small pets, but if you have a busy lifestyle they are time-consuming. They need to be fed and watered daily and regularly cleaned out – a job for poor old dad!

Small birds

Budgies, canaries and small parakeets make excellent house pets, but they do require some looking after. They need a spacious cage and/or access to fly around the room once a day. They need to keep their beaks and claws short and, like all creatures, they need to be fed, watered and regularly cleaned out. Budgies especially make excellent pets and they are very rewarding. They are good mimics, friendly birds and have a decent longevity if cared for properly. Ideally, small birds should be given the run of an aviary, but they are great escape artists and will make a bid for freedom. Unfortunately, most don't fare well in the wild and won't survive for long.

Father Says . . .
Teenagers complain there's nothing to do,
then stay out all night doing it.
BOB PHILLIPS

Dad's Guide to Camping

Whether you're already a seasoned outdoorsman or not, camping is a great way to spend time with your children. It doesn't have to be expensive, it gets you out of the house and into the countryside for a few days. Go on . . . do it! It will do you all good.

If you want a true father-child experience, you can 'rough it' in a small tent, carrying with you all the equipment you need. This might be fine for older children, but don't expect your two-year-old to lug a twenty-pound rucksack on a ten-mile hike to your campsite. For those dads who seriously want to get back to nature, there are campsites that allow you to pretend to be Grizzly Adams. Here you can trek through the countryside, pitch your tent in a woodland clearing and cook your food on an open fire, before scaring your child silly with ghost stories and then trying to get them to sleep. Knowing that there are some civilized facilities not too far away can be a comfort for both you and your child.

If the whole family is going or you'd like a bit more space when you're camping, then a bigger tent is a necessity. Unless

you have a roomy estate car, you might need to consider investing in a trailer or roof rack to transport all the essentials needed to keep the family happy. This may include a fridge or cool box (to keep the milk – and beer – cold), a television (to keep the children quiet on rainy days, and so you can catch up with the football results), as well as games and books to keep the children entertained. Don't worry, most commercial sites have an electric hook-up facility.

If you'd like a little more luxury, then consider a caravan. Yes, you might have to trade in the car if it's a small hatchback, but if you already have a decent-sized family car it should be okay for towing. Towable caravans can be acquired relatively inexpensively but, as with everything else in life, the more you are prepared to spend, the better facilities you get. Modern caravans will comfortably sleep from two to six people, have hot and cold running water, a shower and a toilet. They are perfect for inexpensive family holidays and are far more practical than canvas if the weather conspires against you.

If you don't fancy towing an aluminium box behind your car, a motor home is another option. Containing the same luxuries as a caravan, they are much more expensive and you have to remember to pack everything away before you drive off to the beach for the day.

Father Says . . .
There is nothing wrong with today's teenager
that twenty years won't cure.
ANON

Perils and Pitfalls
of Mobile Phones

Mobile phones are now as much a part of our lives as the television or the computer. However much you may regret the fact that your boss, wife, mother or bank manager can now reach you wherever you may try to seek sanctuary, the mobile phone has made itself indispensable. It comes as no surprise, then, that almost every child aspires to have their own mobile phone. Acquiring their first phone has become something of a rite of passage and the average age at which they join the mobile fraternity has now fallen to just eight. Before you equip your youngster with a mobile, however, there are a number of questions that you really should address.

Mobile-phone marketing companies can 'spam' mobile phones with advertising messages. Tell your child not to use their mobile to enter competitions from where the numbers are harvested. Entering such competitions can also involve a hefty call charge at a premium rate.

Mobile phones can become a 'safety blanket' for children and be relied upon too much for help. Encourage your child to think for themselves and not to phone you up at the first excuse.

Mobile phones can be a distraction when used at inappropriate times. Make sure they turn the phone off when at school, church, the library and other such places. The phone can also be a dangerous distraction when a child is crossing a road or just walking down the street as they are not fully aware of what is going on around them. Pavement reconstruction work, suspicious characters or gangs of youths that your child might otherwise have seen and avoided can be a real danger if a youngster is lost in a phone conversation. Teach your children always to be aware of their surroundings.

Bullying and harassment by other kids can occur through text messaging on mobile phones. Be aware of this problem and ask appropriate questions of your child or your child's teacher if you suspect that anything like this may be happening.

Children may become vulnerable to others wishing to steal the phone or its memory card. Stress the importance of security. They shouldn't go flashing a phone around to show off, and make sure you don't buy them an inappropriately expensive phone (they could start with one of your discards).

Other people can run up bills if the phone is misplaced or stolen. Make sure your child has a pay-as-you-go phone with limited credit.

Children can quickly pick up bad 'textspeak' habits. Keep an eye on their school assignments to ensure they are not using inappropriate abbreviations like 'gr8' for 'great'.

Many believe there may be a radiation health risk to children through overuse of mobile phones. Ensure they are sparing with their phone use and encourage texting as it does not involve holding the receiver to their head.

HINTS

◆ Programme in Mum and Dad's mobile numbers as soon as the new phone is acquired.

◆ Discuss the potential dangers in using phones when in public, crossing roads, etc.

◆ Buy a pay-as-you-go phone and set a budget (e.g. £5 credit per month).

◆ If possible, ensure the phone is protected by a security code (known to you).

◆ Dissuade them from using the phone as a toy or games machine.

◆ Discuss acceptable times and places to use the text-message service.

◆ If on contract, check the numbers called during the billing period, so that you always know the phone is being used
as you would wish it to be.

◆ Enter an ICE (In Case of Emergency) number so that anyone who accesses the phone will know who to call in an emergency.

Ten Classic Board Games

Computer games are all very well, but there's nothing like the classic board games we grew up with for some interactive family fun. During those long winter nights and cold, wet weekends, turn off the telly and rummage in your cupboards for some tried-and-trusted favourites like the ten below. They are a great way to pass the time and, unlike computer games, they also help to get your kids talking to you. Fantastic . . . as long as the game doesn't turn into an argument about who's had their fingers in the till at the Monopoly bank!

1. Yahtzee®
2. Chess
3. Dominos
4. Scrabble
5. Monopoly®

6. Draughts
7. Ludo
8. Trivial Pursuit®
9. Mousetrap®
10. Pictionary

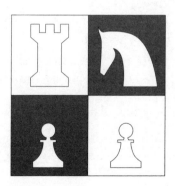

How to Build a Snowman

If you think of snow as the stuff that stops you getting your car out of the drive, stops you getting to work on time, stops you being able to play golf or even stops you wanting to go outdoors, then you need an attitude transplant. Dads need to be able to think like kids. Snow is the stuff that stops you having to go on that dreaded cross-country run, stops the bus from being able to take you to school, stops school from opening at all . . . and stops you wanting to stay indoors!

Go on, admit it, snow makes you feel like a child again. When there's a fresh fall of snow on the ground, all white and sparkly, you really do want to run around in it, make lots of footprints, fall over and make body prints or angel shapes – and have a snowball fight. Most of all, though, when there's enough snow on the ground, anyone who doesn't feel even the twinkling of an urge to build a snowman no longer has any of that spark of childishness left in them. You've lost it, mate.

But don't despair. You can rediscover the child in yourself by joining the kids in the garden or the park to have that snowball fight and build that snowman. Children, of course, will expect you to act as a moving target for their snowballs and be an expert in building a snowman. Wait a minute, though. Have you ever actually built a snowman? In some places it snows so rarely that, even having reached your adult years, you might never have had the opportunity to practise the fine art of constructing a snowman. If that's the case, then here are a few tips.

The simplest kind of snowman is basically just two giant snowballs – a big one for the body and a smaller one for the head.

To start the body, you need to crush together a couple of handfuls of snow, just as you would when making a snowball to throw. Then you need to roll this snowball along the ground, where it will pick up lots more of the white stuff and grow as you roll. If it is extremely cold and the snow is light and fluffy, this could involve more bent-double, back-breaking hard work than if the snow is slightly wetter. The wet snow will stick together better and swell your snowman's body a bit more quickly. If it's too wet, it will just be slush and, sadly, that muck's no good at all.

Roll your snowball in different directions, at different angles, to build a round shape. If you keep rolling only in one direction, the snowball will tend to grow as a cylinder rather than a ball. The more you roll, the bigger the snowball will get and once it is a reasonable size, the kids can join in the pushing.

When the body is as big as you want it, just stop rolling. Now it's time to start on the head. Follow exactly the same procedure for the head, but don't let it get too big. You need to be able to lift the head on to the body and a big snowball gets very heavy. You don't want to do yourself an injury trying to pick the thing up. You can always make the head a bit bigger if needs be by 'plastering' it with snow once you have put it in place on top of the body.

Now that you have the basic snowman shape, all you have to do is add some character. You can make arms from twigs if you can find some under the snow, or you may be able to 'sculpt' arms by adding snow to the body like modelling clay. Whether sculpted arms are made like ridges on the body or can be built sticking out from the body depends very much on how cold the weather is and the quality of your snow.

Traditionally, you would use two lumps of coal for eyes, a carrot for the nose and a line of pebbles to show the mouth. 'Frosty the Snowman' also had a 'corn cob pipe', but you're not likely to have one of those lying around.

Basically, anything that you have to hand that you can push gently into the snowman to create the features will work well enough. The final touch is to dress him in an old hat and scarf.

Now you can go back to round seventeen of the snowball fight!

How to Teach Your Child to Drive

The best tip of all is – hire a driving instructor! That way you are most likely to remain on speaking terms with your child. If you must teach your budding Jenson Button yourself, the following tips may be helpful.

For some reason, teaching someone else to drive (unless you're professionally qualified) often means that rows and recriminations follow. Learn to have patience. It will keep the peace, show your child that you can see they're growing up and becoming responsible and, most importantly, will keep you out of the local A&E suffering from a heart attack or burst blood vessel.

If you do resort to rowing with your offspring, take several deep breaths and remind yourself you're the grown-up. Storming off for two minutes is fine (even if you are being childish) and may calm the situation down. If your child storms off, do not move over to the driving seat, roar off and leave them stranded. Sit calmly and patiently and wait for them to calm down.

Find somewhere vast and safe before you let your teenager sit behind the wheel. An old disused airfield or wasteland is perfect, but it might be easier to choose a quiet street that is relatively free of other traffic. An industrial estate on a Sunday will have very little traffic, besides other pesky learners! Trying to teach a seventeen-year-old hand, eye and foot co-ordination is not easy, but essential if they are going to pass their test and stay safe on the road. They can concentrate far better on practising these basic skills if they don't have any other traffic to worry about.

Explain the controls simply and clearly. Let them start the engine – don't forget to explain about waiting for warning lights to disappear first if you've got a diesel engine – and let them get a feel for the car. To a first-time driver, even the smallest of compact cars feels like a bus, so guide them slowly into finding first gear and remain calm as they jerk their foot off the clutch and knock your head into the windscreen before stalling. It's probably best if you keep your seatbelt on at all times and it's not a bad habit to teach your new learner.

Show no fear

Try again. Eventually, they'll feel that bite, get the hang of it, and before you know it you'll be bumping along in first gear at 30 mph while they grapple around for second. Do not let the fact that your clutch will never be the same again worry you. Most importantly, do not let the driver see your white knuckles as you hold on to the door for dear life while your fingernails draw blood from your palms.

Praise is the key. Encourage all the things they do right and keep the edge out of your voice when they make a mess of it. After a few (painful) sessions, they will have found fourth and fifth gears and if they are able to brake and come to a stop without giving you whiplash, it may be time to try the open road.

Teach your teenager the basics of the car – not just how to start, go and stop. Show them how to put oil in – this involves taking the dipstick out and pointing out that the small hole it has come out of is not where you put the oil in. It's also wise to show them where to pour the windscreen-washer liquid. This does not get splashed down the vents on the bonnet, but actually has its own container in the engine bay. Show them how the petrol cap goes on and off and teach them what to do at the filling station – including paying!

Get help

After a few trips out in the car, your teenager will be starting to feel comfortable driving and it may then be time for you to take a back seat – no, not literally! Unless you are the very best of teachers, your child will now need a professional to coach them through their driving test. Your ideas about the rules of the road may well be years out of date and, while you can provide your child with a basic understanding that will boost their confidence, lessons from a professional are what will bring them the coveted driving licence.

Be prepared to let the novice take the wheel when you go on family visits or on other occasions when you would expect to be driving your child, as the more experience they have behind the wheel, the better.

Then, when your teenager has passed the driving test, you and your partner can look forward to being picked up and chauffeur-driven home after an evening out. The downside of that, of course, is that your car may be 'borrowed' on a regular basis and the gas tank will never have quite as much fuel in it as you thought!

Cards on the Table

If you regularly turn your living room into a suburban version of a Mississippi riverboat for an evening of gambling with a bunch of friends, then you already know how much fun, and how sociable, playing cards can be.

Your partner may not appreciate you teaching gambling games to your children, though, so it may be better (and cheaper) to stick to Knockout Whist and Old Maid when you play with the kids. However, if you can get away with teaching them some gambling games, try Cheat or Pontoon. These are easy to learn and you will probably get as much enjoyment out of the fact that you shouldn't be playing them with seven- or eight-year-olds as you do out of the game itself. The kids will love that, too. If you are gambling, however, play for peanuts – literally. Peanuts or sweets can all be shared out at the end of the game. Don't treat a card session as an opportunity to win back some of the pocket money you've just dished out!

Advanced games

Some of the more complicated games, like Bridge, will be way beyond younger children, but once they have mastered one or two different types of card game, older kids can pick up the more complex games quite quickly.

A trip to the local library will undoubtedly furnish you with a book or books that detail the rules of all of these games and an hour or two of cards on a regular basis will do your children no harm at all. At a basic level it will, in fact, help them with their understanding of numbers and counting, so don't let anyone tell you that you are leading the youngsters astray when you break out the cards.

Choosing a Musical Instrument

You may have been tone deaf all your life and have as much musical talent as your left shoe, but don't let that put you off encouraging your children to take an interest in music. Learning a musical instrument is a slow and, for anyone forced to listen, tortuous process, but it brings all sorts of benefits to your child. While writing music is a hugely creative process, it also involves an orderly logic that has a very close relationship to mathematics. Learning to read music in order to play an instrument is wonderful mind-training for your child. Remind yourself of that when you are sitting with your fingers in your ears during violin or recorder practice at home.

The recorder is the obvious first choice, although boys tend to find this a bit girlie. It's not. It's the grounding that will take them on to learning more difficult instruments and will enable them to read music. There are some clever people around who never learn to read music, those who can just sit down and play. But these are few and far between and, unless your own father is David Bowie, it's unlikely that your child will be born with this kind of natural talent.

Unfortunately, the recorder is a screechy instrument in the wrong hands and most young children are unable to understand the concept of blowing softly. This results in no actual notes, just shrill sheets of sound. Little children also seem incapable of moving their fingers simultaneously and it can be a bit like watching those pop-up games for toddlers where every time something shuts another hole is burst open. Try to remain optimistic and hope they grow out of this instrument and move on to something more mellow.

The piano is also a favourite. Although these can be expensive to buy and maintain, if you're very lucky, someone will be advertising a free one in your local paper, which you can then have tuned. At the other end of the scale, though, you could be looking at spending up to £3,000 on an electronic piano – they don't seem to sell new uprights without electrics these days – although the plus side is that these come with headphones that mean you won't have to listen to hours of relentless scales.

Once your child has mastered the recorder (if you haven't already thrown it out of the window), they might show an interest in the clarinet. Hooray, we hear you shout. But don't get too comfy. This is a difficult instrument to learn. It's not as difficult as something like the oboe, but it still takes time and effort and (on your part) patience.

The flute is a slightly easier wind instrument to master, but as soon as your child has grasped the fingers thing vertically, they'll then have to change finger patterns and hold the instrument horizontally.

Stringed instruments make a beautiful sound. Violins are angelic, while violas are mellow. Cellos resonate with clarity and the double bass is downright funky. The trouble is that it takes a long time to learn how to make them sound their best and that will be stressful on your ears. Children learning the violin are still practising to co-ordinate themselves. The violin requires balancing a bowed stick with horse hair (it's real) over four, fairly close together strings. These are made of fine steel (at least they don't use cat gut any more). This action is quite difficult. To make the job even more difficult, they need to use the fingers on their left hand to make the notes on the fingerboard. This is a feat in itself as there's nothing to tell them where to place their fingers – it's purely practice makes perfect. That's when your ears really start to suffer. The better they get, the more they will be encouraged to wobble said fingers at the same time as making the note. This is called vibrato. You will doubtless come up with a few other names for it.

Brass instruments are no easier to master. Your child will need to learn breath control – that's where the recorder and blowing softly comes in – but you can't blow too softly or there won't be a note at all. Trumpets and cornets are popular, trombones are more difficult, as are French horns.

Percussion is fun, but you need a big house, preferably with a soundproofed barn attached. You will definitely need earplugs if they are learning the drums!

Perhaps the guitar – classical, folk or electric – is for your budding musician. These are reasonable to buy and easily looked after. There are many teachers around who charge competitive rates and you might find the next Eddie Van Halen, Eric Clapton, Jimi Hendrix or even Hank Marvin living in the same house as you!

If the din simply gets too much for you, take a trip to your local pub and drown your sorrows about what might have been, had you stuck it out at your own lessons way back when . . .

Ten Best Threats

You can discuss things with kids; try to persuade them to do something; try to persuade them not to do something; try to reason with them; try to issue them with orders, and try all sorts of arguments to make them do what you want. They can, however, be the most stubborn and defiant creatures ever to walk the face of the earth.

When all else fails, don't be afraid to issue threats – and then don't be afraid to follow through on your threats. Here are ten of the best.

1. 'If you ——— I'll tell your mother when she comes home.'

2. 'If you ——— you'll go to your room and stay there.'

3. 'If you ——— there'll be no more Playstation for the rest of the week.'

4. 'If you ——— I'll take your bike back to the shop.'

5. 'If you ——— you'll be banned from football for the rest of the month.'

6. 'If you ——— you will go to bed early.'

7. 'If you ——— you'll be grounded for a week.'

8. 'If you ——— I'll tell Uncle Dave that you don't deserve to go fishing.'

9. 'If you ——— you won't be allowed sweets/chocolate.'

10. 'If you ——— Santa Claus won't be coming this year.'

How to Survive a Family Holiday

Gone are the days when you could pack a small bag of carry-on baggage and jet off for a couple of weeks in the sun without a care in the world. With a family to worry about, the most restful time of your year can turn out to be the most testing. The only way to make sure it all goes as smoothly as possible is to plan as you pack.

For kids, the excitement of preparing to go on holiday is a high that is tempered only by the extreme low of the boredom of hanging around at an airport or the endless car or train journey to your holiday destination. When you pack your various items of baggage, therefore, you need to bear in mind that you have to make the holiday begin as soon as you leave home.

Be prepared

Give the children a disposable camera each. They'll take lots of pictures of walls, ceilings and floors, but they'll enjoy the independence.

Pack the car the night before, and hide a surprise or two somewhere in the car that kids can search for at rest stops.

Leave home at nap time or better still the early hours. The more your kids sleep in the car, the better for all.

Take a scrapbook, gluestick, pens and scissors; that way they can make a collection of entrance tickets, leaflets and postcards of where they have been during days out.

Don't forget the medical and health-care kit. You can buy these from high-street chemists and, of course, take your own suitable infant painkillers, cough and cold capsules, mosquito repellent and sunscreen. If travelling overseas, check what vaccinations may be required.

Make sure your kids pack a backpack with a few toys, games and books for the journey. Forget any kits that have lots of small pieces, as these will only get lost down the side of the car seat.

Don't do too much too soon! You may want your kids to experience the wonders of Egypt and a transatlantic trip to Disneyland, but take them at an age when they can appreciate what they are seeing and doing.

Kids are usually happiest doing the simplest things. Don't make any trip or visit too complicated or try to cram too much in.

Take a magnifying glass for looking at sea creatures, bugs etc. – just make sure your kids don't know how to start a fire on the holiday-home sofa.

There are many audio tapes available of popular books to entertain during journeys, as well as portable DVD players for favourite films.

Invest in a few pool toys like balls, inflatable alligators or water pistols, which are cheap but can provide hours of fun. You don't even need to bring them home – leave them in the holiday home for the next visitors!

If your children are under school age take advantage of the cheaper holiday prices – they can double during the school holiday period.

Be aware that, after a tiring day out, kids will fall asleep on the homeward journey and will therefore be fully refreshed on arrival, with loads of energy to stay up until at least 2 a.m.

Take plenty of drinks and snacks on a journey but ration them or you'll be stopping for toilet breaks or reaching for a sick bag every few miles.

If there is a kids' holiday club at your hotel or resort, don't feel guilty about leaving your kids there. Children generally love being together with other kids and you are on holiday too, so take the chance of having a breather.

Days out

Avoid disagreements over which tourist spots to visit by allowing each person (parents and children included) to look through the various guides and each choose an attraction. Your kids may not be happy looking around the gardens of an historic house (though you might be okay if you find one with a maze), but at least they know they will be able to choose the water park the next day. If choosing days out causes constant arguments, set up a mystery tour to a destination of your choice. They can try to guess en route where they're going. When you get to the attraction, try letting the kids go into the gift shop before you set off to see the sights. That way they won't be nagging you all day to have a look in the shop.

Don't choose destinations more than an hour's journey away. If it took you seven hours to get to your holiday accommodation, a further journey of whinging, nappy changes, sick bags and endless supply of snacks really isn't worth it.

Try to visit attractions midweek to avoid the crowds.

When going out to restaurants, choose places with a reasonable level of background noise so you're not so conscious of the noise your own kids are making.

Always carry a large tub of wet wipes!

Give older teens some freedom to explore or be on their own. They'll appreciate the space and the opportunity for independence, as well as your confidence in their reliability and behaviour.

Always have a Plan B in case of bad weather or temper tantrums.

Keep a freezer box in the boot and replenish daily with bottles of water, apples and snacks.

When taking your kids on holiday, remember that they will be playing in an unfamiliar environment and that there may be potential hazards.

Children don't always appreciate places and items of special interest, so avoid the headache of them being in a museum and clambering all over a priceless vintage car that doesn't mean a thing to them.

If you've room, take a few board games (though some well-equipped self-catering establishments will have toys, games, videos etc.) that can trigger a wave of nostalgia for parents: junior Monopoly, Frustration, Ker-Plunk, Connect 4, Mousetrap – you know the ones you like (see also page 105).

Carry an emergency bag permanently in the boot with a spare set of clothes and shoes for each child.

Two-family holidays

Going on holiday with another family has its advantages and disadvantages. You may end up never wanting to see the other family ever again, but if you're willing to take the risk, here are some pros and cons to think over.

Having a babysitter on tap is quite useful. At least you can have a few evenings out as a couple, and do the same for your friends.

Having other children around could keep your own entertained.

If possible, think about letting each child travel with each family, swapping over at rest stops.

Extra adults can lessen the responsibility.

Once the kids are in bed, you can have a party!

At least if your friends' children are badly behaved, it will make yours look like little angels.

Differences in child discipline can cause friction. Other people's children never behave as you expect your own to.

You don't know people until you live with them. Be prepared to discover your smashing friends are actually huge pains in the bottom!

The children decide they hate each other.

Competitiveness over how to build the perfect sandcastle or cook the perfect breakfast.

Holiday centres

Instead of a traditional holiday resort or hotel, why not consider a holiday centre, where all your needs may be catered for on one site?

If the centre is self-catering and specifically for families, it will probably provide everything you need, so there's no need to take everything but the kitchen sink with you – it's all already there.

It gives you and the kids a chance to try something different, whether archery, paintballing or horse riding.

Excellent for short breaks, as everything you need is on-site and so you can use your time there efficiently.

The holiday price may be all-inclusive, so you know exactly how much it will cost.

Taking your children abroad

Many of the points already suggested still apply, but note these more specific handy hints:

Once your destination is decided, show the kids where they are going on a globe or atlas.

Dehydration can contribute to jet lag, and airline cabins are notorious for their dry air. Make sure your child gets plenty of fluids during flight time.

Avoid flights that are likely to be full, such as late-afternoon commuter flights and early-morning flights from major hubs.

Consider travelling during low season to beat the crowds and high prices.

Make sure you dress your kids for travel – layers are great, as are shoes that slip on and off with ease.

Before you go, check the climate and take appropriate clothing.

Remember the travel insurance – probably compulsory in most package holidays, however for independent travellers with children it is just as essential.

Try learning the language and teach some simple phrases to the kids.

On the beach

However calm and tranquil a beach may look, there can be hidden dangers.

Check the tide table before going swimming or ask the lifeguard for advice. Find out what warning signs and flags are displayed, know exactly what they mean and ensure that young children are constantly supervised.

Make sure young children know what to do if they lose sight of you and where to go.

At the hotel

When you arrive at your hotel, ask the staff if there are any local hazards such as ponds within the hotel grounds, or nearby cliffs.

Check that the swimming pool is fenced off. Read any safety notices around the pool and obey them. Remember that babies under the age of four months should not be swimming at all, as they will not have had the correct vaccinations.

Examine the stairwells around your hotel room, as they're unlikely to have stair gates.

If you have a room with a balcony, check the height and width of any railings.

Be aware of any sharp-edged furniture in your room.

Make sure you know where the fire exits are located.

In short

◆ Plan ahead.

◆ Perspective – put the holiday into perspective and stop trying to please everyone.

◆ Routine – regardless of the holiday, try to maintain some routine with children.

◆ Moderation – don't go overboard on holiday spending; budget and know your limit.

◆ Selection – pick and choose your holiday activities.

◆ Relax – holidays are meant to be enjoyed by everyone, including dads!

Ten Best Bribes

1. 'If you ———— I'll give you your pocket money early.'

2. 'If you ———— I won't tell your mother.'

3. 'If you ———— I'll buy you a PS3.'

4. 'If you ———— I'll take you bowling on Saturday.'

5. 'If you ———— I'll take you to McDonald's.'

6. 'If you ———— I'll buy you some sweets/chocolate.'

7. 'If you ———— I'll get you *Pirates Of The Caribbean 2*.'

8. 'If you ———— you can stay up late tonight.'

9. 'If you ———— I'll let you go to the party/gig/concert.'

10. 'If you ———— you can invite your friends over on Friday and I'll order pizza.'

Father Says . . .
And my parents finally realize that I'm kidnapped
and they snap into action immediately:
they rent out my room.
WOODY ALLEN

Are We There Yet?

Once you have reached the point where you can't bear to hear the kids desperately trying to make up yet another verse to 'The Wheels On The Bus' (*The one-legged giraffe with a sore throat on the bus goes* . . . is probably the limit), you can try a few games.

Many of the games you can play in the car are probably games you played as a kid, but have forgotten all about. Bear in mind these games are also great for when you are in airport departure lounges or waiting for a table in a restaurant; they don't have to be solely for the car.

Here are ten top games for the car.

1 Twenty Questions

The game of Twenty Questions is a true classic that can be played by children of all ages. There are many variations of the game.

One person thinks of something that falls under the category of animal, mineral or vegetable and then tells the other players which category is correct. The players then take turns asking questions which can be answered with a YES or NO. For instance, if the category is animal, a player might ask 'Can it fly?' or 'Does it have four legs?' And after twenty questions are asked, if the players have not already guessed the answer, each player gets a last chance to make a guess. Afterwards, a new player tries to stump the group.

2 Geography

Geography is not for younger children. This game is best for children aged eight and up. Not only do they enjoy the game, they know enough locations to be able to play the game well. Although the finer points may vary from place to place, this is how the basic game is played.

Someone starts by naming a country such as Japan. The next person must name a country whose name begins with the last letter of the previously named country. In this case, Japan ends in N, so a country which begins with N must be named, such as Nigeria. Then, since Nigeria ends in an A, the next person's country must start with an A. And so on, until someone gets stumped – they then drop out and the ritual recommences until just one of you is left as winner.

❸ What's My Name?

A simple, yet fun game and perfect for children of all ages. Think of a name. Then tell the group whether it is a boy's or girl's name, and tell them the first letter of the name. The group then tries to guess the name by calling out all the names they can think of which start with the appropriate letter. That's it. Simple, but fun!

❹ Alphabet Memory Game

Good for children of all ages. An excellent way to help reinforce a preschooler's ABCs, yet fun for the primary school-age child too!

The first person starts with the letter A and says 'A is for —' filling in the blank with any word beginning with the letter A, such as APPLE, ARTICHOKE or AEROPLANE. Let's use APPLE. The second person then does the letter B, but must also remember what A was! So, let's say the second person decides to use the word BOOK for B, the second person would say, 'A is for APPLE and B is for BOOK.'

You continue through the alphabet. By the time you get up to the letter Z, the player will have to recite each and every letter with its corresponding item. The game takes a while and kids love it, particularly if you throw in some silly words or phrases like S is for SMELLY TOES.

5 I Spy

The object of the game is to announce something that you spy (see) and have someone guess the correct answer.

It should be something you can see constantly, like the sky, or Dad's glasses, or the truck in front of you – not something that you pass quickly on the road.

To start the game, you say aloud, 'I spy with my little eye something beginning with "M".'

Have people ask you yes or no questions, one at a time, such as: 'Is it Mummy?' or 'Is it Dad's moustache?'

Whoever guesses the correct answer gets the next turn to spy.

You can simplify this to 'I spy the colour blue', for younger travellers, inspiring questions such as: 'Is it the sky?' or 'Is it my jumper?'

6 All About You

This is a good game to play when the sun goes down and you can't see much out of your car window.

Ask thoughtful questions of everyone in the car. Then take the time to listen to the answers and then discuss them.

It's a great way to learn more about the people you are travelling with!

Here are some questions you can ask to get started.

'If you could have lunch with any three people in the world, alive or not, who would they be and why?'

'If you won £1 million on the Lottery, what would you do with it?'

7 Guess The Number

Let your child think of a number in a stated range of numbers. You then try to guess the number by asking questions. Here's an idea of how it might go:

Your child: 'I'm thinking of a number between 1 and 100.'

You ask: 'Is it more than 50?'

Your child: 'No.'

You: 'Is it an even number?'

Child: 'No.'

You: 'Can you divide this number into three equal parts?'

And so forth.

After you have guessed the number, let your child guess a number that you are thinking of by asking similar questions.

One benefit of this game is that, by asking questions about numbers, it helps your child to develop an understanding of some concepts, characteristics and meanings of numbers. If they find it difficult at first, this is an opportunity to explain and help them understand.

8 Red Car, Yellow Car, Blue Car . . .
Ask the children to choose a colour or model of car of their choice. Set a timescale of ten or fifteen minutes, during which they have to mark down how many cars they see of their chosen colour or model.

9 Who Am I?
Think of someone famous and give the other players a clue. For example, Elvis Presley could be hinted at by the description 'singer' or the initials EP. The others take turns to guess who you are. Once the famous person has been guessed, the winner chooses the next celebrity.

10 What's My Job?
You will need to think of a profession, say a dentist, farmer or train driver, and give the players ten chances to guess your job by taking it in turn to ask questions. You can give an action of what the job is as a clue, as long as you're not driving! The winner has the next go at choosing a profession.

Ten Things Fathers Wish They'd Known

1. I wish I'd known what to expect. Maybe then I'd have all the right answers at just the right moments!

2. I wish I'd known that I should have written down all the hilarious things they said.

3. I wish I'd learned how to balance the art of listening and the desire to solve. Don't tell the children exactly the 'right' answer before they've finished telling their problem.

4. I wish I'd treasured the special moments of laughing, wrestling and telling silly stories.

5. I wish I'd known it takes about thirty-five minutes to clean play dough off the floor, about forty-five minutes to get crayon marks off the wall, and about a week to remove any mark if combined with paint.

6. I wish I'd known what to do when the disposable nappies ran out in the middle of a park on a beautiful summer day.

7. I wish I'd known that a smile ALWAYS helps.

8. I wish I'd known how to stay awake at Monday night Scout meetings and Saturday morning soccer practice.

9. I wish I'd known that children might listen to words but pay more attention to actions.

10. I wish I had realized that fatherhood is not something that can be acted, rehearsed, or imagined, but must be experienced every moment of each and every day.

Famous Fathers

It's always good to be able to remind your kids of how important fathers are, especially in the run-up to Father's Day. You may already be incredibly successful or famous, a respected businessman or captain of industry, an award-winning sportsman or major figure in the arts – but to your kids you're just Dad.

To your child, of course, you are the most important Dad ever to have walked the face of the planet, but if he or she ever doubts how vital fathers have been throughout history, here are a few examples to floor them with.

Father of modern computing – Alan Turing
At the time of his death in 1954, brilliant boffin Alan Turing had already played a major role in the development of the intelligent computer. Headstrong, eccentric and prone to solitary pursuits, Turing distinguished himself as a brilliant mathematician at King's College Cambridge, and, later, at Princeton began work on proofs that established the foundation of the British computer.

Father of modern science – Albert Einstein
German-born Albert Einstein was still in his twenties when he discovered new factors in the relation between water and energy. When he was twenty-six years old he thought out his theory of relativity and light. After some time, he wrote a book called *The Year Book of Physics.* He completed his famous formulation $E=MC^2$ after he had a physical and nervous collapse and was sick for weeks. He published another book which established the theory for and potential effects of the splitting of the atom. The information from the books gave people the

idea of the atom bomb, although Einstein never wanted his work used in that way.

Father of freedom – Nelson Mandela

Nelson Mandela grew up in South Africa under the apartheid system of government which discriminated against non-white citizens. Starting out as a leader of an underground political movement called the African National Congress (ANC), Mr Mandela played a part in many dramatic demonstrations against the white-ruled government. His career in the ANC was cut short in 1964 when he was sentenced to life in prison. But even then, Mandela continued to be a beacon of hope for his people who carried on the struggle in his absence. In 1990, after twenty-seven years of imprisonment, Mandela was freed. His release marked the beginning of the end for apartheid.

Father of modern biology – Charles Darwin

Charles Darwin did not dream up the idea of evolution, he was merely the first to put forward an explanation of how evolution worked in a way that explained what he and other biologists saw in the world. Darwin developed the theory of Natural Selection. This is the idea that the environment an organism lives in helps to determine which organisms survive and produce young, and which do not.

In 1859, Darwin published *On The Origin of Species*, a book which sold out the first day it was in print. It was also an immediate source of great controversy.

Father of comedy – Charlie Chaplin

Charlie Chaplin was an English comedy actor, considered to be one of the finest mimes and clowns ever caught on film. Chaplin began in the silent-film era and acted in, directed,  scripted, produced, and eventually even scored his own films. His working life in entertainment spanned over seventy years, from the British Victorian stage and music hall in England as a child performer until his death at the age of eighty-eight. He led one of the most remarkable and colourful lives of the twentieth century, from a Dickensian London childhood to the pinnacle of world fame in the film industry.

Father of rock'n'roll – Elvis Presley

Elvis Aron Presley was an American singer and actor regarded by many as the greatest entertainer of the twentieth century. He was the most commercially successful singer of rock'n'roll after bursting onto the scene in 1954, but he also had success with ballads, country, gospel, blues, pop, folk and even semi-operatic and jazz standards. In a musical career of over two decades, Presley set many records for concert attendance, television ratings and sales of recordings, becoming one of the best-selling artists in music history.

Father of children's books – A. A. Milne

Alan Alexander (also known as A. A.) Milne, was a British author and playwright. He is most famous for his Pooh books about a boy named Christopher Robin, based on his son, and various characters inspired by his son's stuffed animals, most notably the bear named Winnie-the-Pooh. A Canadian black bear named Winnie (after Winnipeg), which was the military mascot of the Royal Winnipeg Rifles, a Canadian infantry regiment in World War I, was left to London Zoo after the war and is presumed to be the source of the name. E. H. Shepard illustrated the original Pooh books, using his own son's teddy, Growler ('a magnificent bear'), as the model. Christopher Robin Milne's original toys are now in a New York collection.

Father of puppeteers – Jim Henson

James Maury Henson was the best known American puppeteer in modern American television history as well as a film director, and television producer. He was the creator of the Muppets (the name a cross between marionette and puppet) and the leading force behind their long creative run. Henson brought his engaging cast of characters, innovative ideas, and sense of timing and humour to millions. He is also widely acknowledged for the ongoing vision of faith, friendship, magic and love which infused his work. Television shows *The Muppets* and *Sesame Street* thrilled millions of children, including his own, who now carry on his tradition.

Father of football – Pelé

'I was born for soccer, just as Beethoven was born for music.' These are the words of Edson Arantes do Nascimento, the Brazilian genius known throughout the football world as Pelé, who burst onto the scene as a teenager in the late 1950s. A veteran of four World Cups, scorer of 1,283 first-class goals (twelve of them in World Cup final tournaments) and a member of those magical Brazilian squads that won soccer's greatest prize in 1958, 1962 and 1970, Pelé remains the undisputed King of Soccer. He ended his career in the United

States where his presence gave the game a much-needed boost

Father of explorers – Christopher Columbus

Columbus's voyages of discovery to the Americas launched the European colonization of the New World. While history places great significance on his first voyage of 1492, he did not actually reach the mainland of North America until his third voyage in 1498. Likewise, he was not the earliest European explorer to reach the Americas, as there are accounts of European transatlantic contact prior to 1492. Nevertheless, Columbus' voyage came at a critical time of growing national imperialism and economic competition between developing nation states seeking wealth from the establishment of trade routes and colonies. The anniversary of his landing in the New World (Columbus Day) is celebrated throughout the Americas as well as in Spain and Italy, the USA choosing the second Monday in October to mark the occasion.

Father Says . . .
A father is someone who carries pictures in his wallet where his money used to be.
ANON

Ten Things to Know by Heart

As a dad you will sometimes have questions fired at you by schoolteachers, scout masters or doctors that will leave you flapping your lips like a thirsty fish. You just won't have the answers and will look like you know next to nothing about your own child.

Here are some things you should know by heart about your child and some things you can settle for just knowing where to look them up. Do yourself a favour and only clutter your mind with the bits of information that you need. This means information that you need for safety reasons and answers to questions that, if you get them wrong, will make you look like an idiot.

1. Your child's full name — Duh . . .
2. Your child's date of birth — You will be asked to fill this out more times than you may think.
3. Your child's allergies — You obviously don't want to feed a peanut to a child who is allergic to them.
4. The current favourite food.
5. The current favourite bedtime toy or story.
6. Your child's doctor's name and location. In case of emergency it will be important to relay this information to the hospital.
7. Your child's current weight. This is very important when, at three in the morning, they have a fever and you need to know what the correct medicine dosage is.
8. What your child is wearing today. This is important in the scary but unlikely chance you need to describe your child to the police should he or she have gone missing.
9. What things scare your child.
10. Your child's best friends' names.

Step Families
and How to Survive Them

Other people's kids can be a dad's absolute worst nightmare. If they misbehave when you're in charge, you feel awkward talking sharply to them, you're not sure how to discipline them, you don't want them running off to tell tales about how you threatened to strangle them . . . and they know it. So how on earth do you cope when you discover that the woman you have fallen for comes with a brood attached?

Some say living in harmony with your partner's children is the ultimate challenge, more risky than stomping through a minefield with dustbin lids strapped to your feet. It's a treacherous emotional jungle, fraught with danger, fights, tantrums and misunderstandings – and that's just for you. For the kids, it's even worse. If you've got a sense of humour, keep it on stand-by at all times. If you haven't, go out and get one – quick.

You're not the enemy
The key to a successful step-family and all the added extras that go with it are communication, respect, understanding and the ability to listen. You will also need to acknowledge the problems that they may face, not just the obvious ones, but the feelings of insecurity, abandonment and confusion. Not easy, especially when you are faced with kids that think you're an impostor, or worse still, the enemy. You're not, of course, but showing them you're not will be difficult.

There will probably be two sides to this. The kids you have moved in with and the ones that are your own. It is imperative that all the children feel that your house is their home, whether they live with you full-time or part-time. You don't want your own kids feeling like 'guests' when they come to stay. The object is to provide a happy, stable home where everyone is loved equally and where the children's 'issues', should there be any, can be heard and acknowledged. Meanwhile, you rack your brains for a workable solution to any problems that come up and then wait for your partner to sort them out.

You won't be able to do this on your own. You and your partner need to be in it together. As well as trying to walk on a tightrope with the children you will probably be finding your feet in your new relationship. Take time out (yeah, right), to be with each other. The stronger you are together, the more likely it is that your family will start to gel.

Cruel comments

Ignore snide or hurtful remarks from the children – you are being tested. Ex-spouses often have an awful lot to say when you find a new partner and family. Unforgivably, these types of remarks are often passed to your children to pass on to you. It's meant to hurt (they're jealous). It's meant to undermine your new-found happiness (yep, they're still jealous). Don't let it bother you. Ignore it and, whatever you do, don't slate your ex in front of any of the children. Wait until they are tucked up in bed, or, if older, have gone round to their mates' to listen to the latest Lostprophets album and then grab your partner, take a case of wine (one bottle won't be enough) and vent your spleen until you can barely stand and your partner gently guides you to bed.

Make sure, though, that one of you is able to collect the kids not yet home – you don't want to give any ammunition to the opposition. Thankfully, not all step-families face hostility from ex-partners and if you can all be adult about the situation it's the children who benefit most.

Do things together

Try to find activities that all the family will enjoy. If you've got one, walk the dog. Go to the cinema, go bowling – do anything, but try to do it together. Letting all the kids in your life pelt you with snowballs or soak you with water pistols is great for bonding. Take them to a local wood or forest and help them climb trees – being careful to remain underneath, just in case. When it's your turn, throw yourself out of a suitable tree. Mind you, if you're a father of a certain age or prone to accidents, it's probably better to feign this.

At the same time, try to take time out with all the children individually. You need to show both your own children and those new in your life that you value them on their own. Children whose parents separate often have low self-esteem and low self-worth. Show them that, despite the hardships of life and the confusion of new relationships, they are special, loved and cared about. Hopefully, if you can achieve a healthy balance in their lives, you might one day hear words from your step-child that will melt your heart: 'I love you.'

Father Says . . .
You can tell a child is growing up when he stops
asking where he came from and starts refusing
to tell where he is going.
ANON

What's in the Attic?

There's nothing in the attic but spiders and dust and useless old junk, right? Wrong! Well, there may be plenty of spiders and dust but you can bet that old junk isn't all useless, it's a treasure trove! Crawling around in the musty room upstairs searching for hidden gems is well worth the effort, unless you happen to live in an apartment block, in which case the neighbours who live above might not be too pleased. But even if you don't have an attic, your parents probably do, and having a rummage can bring back all sorts of memories of your childhood that you can share with your kids.

Here are our Top Ten finds that will have you reminiscing about the good old days – now get out that stepladder and see what you can find.

1 The train set or Scalextric set that used to be your favourite toy, but you were only allowed to play with on special occasions because your mum didn't like it cluttering the house.

2 The bike you first learned to ride on, hanging on for dear life as your dad pushed you down a hill so that you could 'learn to balance'!

3 The box of old family photographs that your mum used to bring out every so often to make you cringe, but which now fills you with nostalgia.

4 The trophy you won playing for your junior school football team.

5 The piles and piles of school books that your mum hasn't quite got to throwing out yet . . . even though you left school all of twenty years ago!

6 Your old Cub uniform.

7 The Dinky toys you now wished you had been more careful with because they'd be worth an absolute fortune these days.

8 Your old computer games that now make you feel old because you can see exactly how far technology has advanced.

9 The complete set of *Famous Five* and *Secret Seven* books that you loved reading as a boy. Give them to your kids, they will love them too!

10 Your old vinyl (yes, remember vinyl?) albums and singles. In this digital age, how many people still have a turntable? If you do, then stick your records on and relive your youth!

Teenage Talk

Understanding what your teenager is saying, when you can actually get him to talk to you, can be a real trial. Here are a few words and phrases to try to help you communicate, but remember that this is for reference only – don't try to 'get down' with the kids', it never works!

bait obvious, as in 'that's so bait'

bare a lot of, very

beast something that's really cool

book cool – from the first option given in predictive text when trying to type c-o-o-l

buff sexy, fit

bum to enjoy something – to really like something is to 'bum it blue', but 'he bummed it black' means he used to like it, but has since gone off it

butters ugly (pronounced without sounding the 't's)

buzzing cool

chirps chat up, as in 'We chirps some buff gals last night'

chung extremely sexy. If someone is described as 'chung', he or she is better-looking than their 'buff' friend

clappin' out of date or worn out. Usually used to describe attire or accessories, as in 'man, my tracksuit is clappin''

cotch down to hang out, relax, chill out or sleep

crump a multi-purpose term which generally means bad, but can also mean good, depending on the context: 'that ain't good, man, it's crump' or 'that's one crump message you left there'

dash to pass something to somebody, including to throw violently with intent to damage

dred dreadful, terrible, bad, cruel

dry dull, boring, stupid, unfunny – a bad joke might be described as 'dry'

feds police – taken from the US word for the FBI

flat roofin' to be overworked and stressed, as in 'I was flat roofin' for my exams'

fo sho 'urban' version of yes, for sure, certainly

from ends one who is 'from the streets' and knows what's going on

fudge a very, very stupid person indeed, the implication being that these letters will be their exam results

grimy good, or may describe a practical joke or amusing, probably unsavoury, act

hangin' ugly, most likely with an unattractive body and bad dress sense to boot

heavy cool, interesting

howling ugly

jack to steal or take, as in 'carjacking'

jokes funny or enjoyable, as in 'that party was jokes'

jook to stab or to steal

kotch sit and chill out. See also cotch

laoy dat forget that

lush good-looking, sexy

mint cool

munter ugly – an alternate to 'minger', which has long since passed into the mainstream since its first recorded use in 1995

nang London term for cool, excellent, brilliant – when something is very good, it's 'proper nang'

nim nim nim blah blah blah; yadda yadda yadda – what's said when someone is talking rubbish

off the hook cool, appealing, fresh, exceeding expectations

rago whatever, OK

random odd, irregular, crazy

rents parents

rinsed used up, all gone

roll with hang out with

safa coolest of the cool, superlative version of safe (see below)

safe cool, good, sweet

shabby cool, smart, as in 'that's a well shabby suit.'

sick interesting, cool, never seen before – the more sick something is, the better

sik *see* sick

slap to beat up

swag once denoted ill-gotten gains and then freebies, particularly branded merchandise

switch to turn on someone

tell over

told over to rat on someone

unass to surrender control of an object or person

vexed irritated, angry

wagwaan what's up, what's going on?

wicked cool – yes, it has made a comeback!

Top Ten Gadgets for Dads

If your offspring are stuck for 'crump' present ideas, leave this book conveniently open at this page. Make sure you do this well in advance of your birthday, Christmas or Father's Day, or it'll be socks and hankies again!

1. Slippies microwavable foot warmers

2. Motorized coin sorter

3. Sim card back-up keyring

4. Homer Simpson talking beer-bottle opener

5. Digital alcohol tester

6. Battery-powered heated gloves

7. MY Q brain builder

8. Jack Daniels gourmet coffee and mug

9. Ozone inflatable lounger

10. Sat Nav system

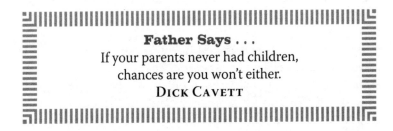

Father Says . . .
If your parents never had children,
chances are you won't either.
DICK CAVETT

Dad's Dream Cars

Bored with driving your family saloon or people carrier? Why not sit back and take a little time to fantasize about the car you *really* want to be seen driving! Unless you're absolutely loaded, you're about as likely ever to get your hands on one as you are to win total control of the TV remote. One of the best things about them is most of them have absolutely no room for the kids.

Ferrari Enzo

You know it's never going to become a reality and that's why this tops the list. Ferarri only made 349 of these cars and, even if you'd just won the lottery, they decided who was worthy of buying them. The 6-litre V12 engine produces 660 bhp (brake horse power), allowing you to go from 0–60 in 3.65 seconds. The £425,000 Enzo has a top speed of 218 mph and even has a button that lifts the nose of the car up so you won't damage your pride and joy going over a speed bump . . .

Mercedes SLR Maclaren

If you want to feel a bit like James Bond, then this is the car for you. You enter the SLR through beetle-wing doors and spark the car into action by flipping the top of the gear knob to expose the starter button. It's 5.5-litre V8 supercharged engine produces 626 bhp, giving a 0–60 figure of 3.6 seconds and a top speed of 208 mph. With a production run of 3,500, it is slightly more accessible than the Enzo, but the price tag of nearly £320,000 – and the fact anyone over six-feet tall will find it almost impossible to drive – may well put you off.

Lamborghini Murcielago

Lamborghini is a name synonymous with dream cars: almost every boy has dreamed about driving one. The Murcielago is the latest to roll off the production line (if not trip off the tongue!) and, at a mere £168,000, is far more gentle on the wallet. The 6.2 litre V12 produces 575 bhp, does 0–60 in 3 seconds and gives a top speed of 205 mph. There's a rear spoiler that automatically angles to 50 degrees at 81 mph and 70 degrees at 137 mph, by which time that police traffic car will be just a dot in the rear view mirror!

Aston Martin Vantage

Unveiled at the 2005 Geneva Motor Show, the Vantage has been labelled the 'must-have sports car'. It's easy to see why when you look at the impressive performance figures: 0–60 in 4.8 seconds, and with a top speed of 175 mph. How can you put a price on seeing your friend's faces when you say, 'My other car's an Aston Martin'? But, at 'just' £82,800, it is far more affordable than many of the cars featured here. With a V8 quad-cam 32-valve engine that is hand assembled, this really is one of the ultimate muscle cars . . . and it's small enough to fit in your garage!

Porsche Carrera GT

Originally intended to dominate the Le Mans 24-hour race, rule changes made the Carrera GT ineligible so it was the driving public who benefited. Porsche have developed a 7-litre V10 engine that creates a monstrous 612 bhp and a top speed of 208 mph. It costs £325,000, does 0–60 in 3.9 seconds and will take less than ten seconds to hit 124 mph. At only 46 inches high, it'll look good on your drive, even if you struggle to get in it!

Pagani Zonda F

Dedicated to the memory of legendary F1 driver Juan Manuel Fangio, the rear wheel drive Zonda F boasts a 7.3 litre V12 engine that produces over 600 bhp. It flies to 60 mph in 3.8 seconds and will do over 210 mph flat out. Futuristic carbon-fibre construction means it weighs about the same as a medium-sized family hatchback, but that's where the comparison ends as it costs around £380,000.

TVR Tuscan S

If you want a pure driving experience at a realistic budget, then plump for the TVR Tuscan S. Although it does boast an electrically-assisted steering rack and firmer suspension, it doesn't waste time with the needless niceties of traction control, anti-lock brakes or airbags – an approach which allows the car to hit a very respectable 175 mph. Add in a 0–60 time of 4.6 seconds and the £49,995 price tag begins to look more reasonable.

Lotus Sport Exige 240R

As *Top Gear* presenter Jeremy Clarkson pointed out while test-driving the Ferrari Enzo, if Lotus gave one of their cars their founder's first name this could be called the Colin! The Lotus name evokes images of sports cars that will transport you back to your childhood. The Exige 240R has a finely-tuned 1.8 litre engine that produces 243 bhp and a top speed of 155 mph. At £44,000 and with the ability to reach 60 mph in a

staggering 3.9 seconds, every father should have one for when they need some quiet time on their own . . .

Ford GT

For those of you with a nostalgic side, the Ford GT's retro styling will suit you perfectly. It has a supercharged V8 engine that produces 550 bhp and a top speed of 205 mph. You'll be able to leave your rivals standing at the lights with an extremely impressive 0–60 time of 3.3 seconds. Cost is not *that* prohibitive either, the GT being priced around £75,000. The trouble is that Ford are only going to manufacture 4,200 of these cars and demand will be high.

Hummer H2

If you have to imagine yourself in one car that can easily accommodate a family, then this is it. For those fathers who still have a yearning to play soldier, the military-styled Hummer H2 is the car for you. While not the perfect vehicle for the school run – it's enormous, and fuel consumption diminishes to practically nothing when you put your foot down – a 16-inch wall will prove no obstacle for the H2. It's powered by a 6-litre V8 and labours to 60 mph in over 10 seconds, but once you get up to a reasonable speed it's perfect for cruising the motorways.

How to Teach Your Child to Dive

There's nothing more flashy than a perfectly executed, graceful dive into the holiday swimming pool, and nothing more embarrassing than a painful belly flop that sprays everyone with water and rips your trunks off. Make sure you are capable of the graceful version before you start trying to teach your child to dive.

You must also make sure that the pool is suitable for diving. If it's too shallow, you are likely to emerge covered in blood and snot with a broken nose. Many pools have 'No Diving' notices for this very reason – hitting the bottom can cause serious injuries.

So, providing that you are sure that the pool, or the sea if you are diving off a jetty or rock, is deep enough, you can try showing your youngster how it's done. Once they are confident swimmers, kids love jumping into pools or the sea, and it comes quite naturally to them. Diving, however, is something that can take a while to master. Going in head first is not as simple as hitting the water bottom first. Children have to be good swimmers before trying this, though, as they should never dive while wearing arm bands, any kind of flotation aid or any encumbrances such as face masks or snorkels. Proper swimming goggles are okay.

Show how it's done

The first thing to do is to demonstrate your dive. Make sure that you show them how to stand at the edge of the pool properly. Your toes should be able to curl over the edge and your balance should be on the balls of your feet. Then bend your knees and lean forward from the waist, duck your head down

and bring your arms up so that your hands will hit the water first.

Spring off the side and straighten your legs behind you. After hitting the water, push your head back and arch your back so that you swoop back to the surface still facing away from the edge.

The forward roll

Your child can't be expected to get all of that right first time, so start him or her off from a crouched position so that he or she can 'roll' forwards into the water. Make sure that your pupil straightens up in the water, though, because you don't want them to produce a complete forward roll and risk banging their head against the side. You should be in the water when supervising this training to make sure that does not happen. When performing this 'roll', the arms should still be held out in front of the head to break the water first.

From the crouch, you can progress to standing slightly more erect, always ensuring that your pupil achieves a 'swoop' in the water to take them away from the edge.

Now you need to encourage the flexing of the knees to give a little spring to the dive and force the legs up behind. You should be telling them to try to arc like a rainbow through the air and imagine a square patch on the surface of the water that they should aim to hit with their hands.

With a bit of practice, a child who is already comfortable with jumping in and swimming, will soon master the dive and, doubtless, be telling *you* where you're going wrong.

Father Says . . .
Children really brighten up a household –
they never turn the lights off.
RALPH BUS

Dads on the Touchline

When your son or daughter starts taking part in competitive sports, whether it be tennis, football, rugby, hockey, basketball, athletics or any other team game, you will be expected not only to ferry them to and from the event, but also to show the proper kind of support during the match.

Your child will appreciate your presence, but not if you make a complete twit of yourself, so don't embarrass them by getting overexcited. Here are a few 'dos' and don'ts' for attending your offspring's sporting fixtures.

1. Do bring an umbrella if you're going to be outside. Obviously an umbrella is going to look pretty stupid at an indoor basketball or volleyball game.

2. Don't question the referee's parentage.

3. Do applaud the team, not just your own child. Your youngster wants to be part of the team, not constantly singled out by a bawling father.

4. Don't shout, 'Break his leg, son!'

5. Do stand well away from the action to avoid flying balls/players. Your child does not want to have to take an injured parent to hospital after the game.

6. Don't make loud comments about the manager or coach's IQ, physique or sexual orientation if he keeps your child on the subs' bench.

7. Do stand with other parents of children in your son/daughter's team and don't get into fracas with the opposition's parents.

8 Don't hug any of the other parents present.

9 Do stress the values of the game. Play to win, but play with respect and if you don't win, be a sporting loser.

10 Don't invade the pitch and join in the goal celebrations.

The Laugh's on You

Fathers are expected to come out with some cheesy lines. So here's a few to get you going. In fact, you may have heard a few of these yourself from your own dad!

Whenever you come home from work and sit at an empty plate, flip your tie onto it and say, 'I don't know about you, but I'm having Thai tonight.'

Playfully (and gently!) boot your boy's backside, and when he turns around with a look of indignation, say, 'Nice to see I can still make an impression.'

At the New Year's Eve party, it's two minutes past midnight and you say, 'I haven't had a drink all year.'

When there's fruit on the go and you're asked if you'd like a pear, you always say, 'No thanks, just one will do.'

When someone coughs, you say, 'It's not the cough that carries you off, it's the coffin they carry you off in.'

When you are asked to put on your kid's shoes, you say, 'But they won't fit me.'

Whenever you hear the name Isabelle mentioned,
you say, 'Isabelle necessary on a bike?'

Whenever you hear the name Mary mentioned,
you say, 'Ho-ho-ho . . . Mary Christmas.'

When asked to pay for something or dish out the pocket
money, you pull some notes from your wallet and say,
'But these are my favourite beer vouchers.'

When that bottle-of-wine-shaped present is handed to you
at Christmas, you say, 'Don't tell me . . . it's a book.'

Whenever you are asked if you are having trouble hearing,
you say, 'Eh?'

If you are caught talking to yourself, you say, 'It's the only
way I can get a decent conversation around here.'

When your child wants something to eat and says,
'I'm hungry,' you say, 'I'm Germany, pleased to meet you.'

When driving past some black-and-white cows, you say, 'Boy,
it must be cold out there . . . those cows are Friesian!'

At dinner, when the meat is placed in front of you to carve, you say, 'Well, here's my dinner . . . what are the rest of you going to eat?'

✻

On a car journey when you are asked, 'Where are we, Dad?' you say, 'In the car.'

✻

As your child leaves to go out and says, 'I'm off', you say, 'I wondered what the smell was!'

✻

When phone starts ringing, you say, 'That'll be the phone', and then, 'If it's for me, don't answer it.'

✻

Whenever you are offered a doughnut, you sing, 'Doughnut forsake me, oh, my darling . . .'

✻

When your child wants something to drink and says, 'I'm thirsty', you say, 'Hi, I'm Friday!'

✻

If your partner asks you to put the kettle on, you say, 'I don't think it will fit.'

✻

If you are asked to 'put the cat out', you say, 'I didn't realise it was on fire.'

When you are asked if you caught the train/bus, you say,
'No, my net wasn't big enough.'

Should someone ever ask, 'Where's the paper?' you say,
'In the cupboard beside the salt.'

If you are forced to answer the phone you pick it up saying,
'It's the garden ornament . . . hello, statue?'

Whenever you take your shoes off, you waggle them
in front of your face, sing some rubbish and say,
'That's sole music for you.'

Upon hearing someone in a restaurant dropping glasses
or crockery, you say, 'Sack the juggler!' or 'That's smashing!'
or, like Long John Silver's parrot, 'Pieces of plate!
Pieces of plate!'

On entering anywhere that has stuffed and mounted animal
heads on display, you say, 'It must have been going pretty fast
to come straight through that wall!'

At the Greek Restaurant, the waiter hands you the menu,
and you say, 'Can you recommend something?
This menu's all Greek to me.'

The waiter mentions one of the specials tonight is chicken, and you say, 'None for me . . . it's foul!'

✱

When being offered a hot towel in a Chinese restaurant, you say, 'No thank you, I'm full!'

✱

The waiter recommends the duck and you say, 'As long as I don't get the bill.'

✱

When eating mushrooms, you must always say that you'd like to eat more but you don't have mush room.

✱

When any child puts ketchup on their plate, you say, 'Do you want some food to go with your ketchup?'

✱

After a large meal, you say, 'Well that was a nice starter, now what's for dinner?'

✱

When a child asks, 'Please may I leave the table?' you say, 'Well, you weren't thinking of taking it with you were you?'

✱

When a very polite child asks, 'Please may I get down from the table?' you say, 'You don't get down from the table . . . you get down from a duck.'

After a meal you say, 'Good thing we ate when we did, because I'm not a bit hungry now.'

*

If your child moans, 'Well it's just not fair!' you say, 'Well it's just not raining . . .'

*

When you are asked, 'Is it Wednesday today?' you say, 'All day . . .'

*

If a child asks, 'Dad, can you put my shirt on?' you say, 'Sure, I can put it on the dog.'

*

When anyone asks, 'Can you call me a taxi?' you say, 'Of course . . . you're a taxi.'

*

When a child is poking around in his or her ear, you say, 'Never put anything in your ear sharper than your elbow.'

*

If you are asked, 'Dad, can you pick me up tonight?' you say, 'As long as you don't put on any more weight.'

*

Mum says, 'Can you make me a cup of coffee?' and you wave your hand over her head and say, ' Abracadabra! You are now a cup of coffee.'